Ghosts of
West Chester, Pennsylvania

Mark Sarro

4880 Lower Valley Road, Atglen, Pa 19310

Ouija® is a registered trademark of Parker Brother's Games

Schiffer Books are available at special discounts for bulk purchases for sales promotions or premiums. Special editions, including personalized covers, corporate imprints, and excerpts can be created in large quantities for special needs. For more information contact the publisher:

Published by Schiffer Publishing Ltd.
4880 Lower Valley Road
Atglen, PA 19310
Phone: (610) 593-1777; Fax: (610) 593-2002
E-mail: Info@schifferbooks.com

For the largest selection of fine reference books on this and related subjects, please visit our web site at
www.schifferbooks.com
We are always looking for people to write books on new and related subjects. If you have an idea for a book please contact us at the above address.

This book may be purchased from the publisher.
Include $5.00 for shipping.
Please try your bookstore first.

You may write for a free catalog.

In Europe, Schiffer books are distributed by
Bushwood Books
6 Marksbury Ave.
Kew Gardens
Surrey TW9 4JF England
Phone: 44 (0) 20 8392-8585; Fax: 44 (0) 20 8392-9876
E-mail: info@bushwoodbooks.co.uk
Website: www.bushwoodbooks.co.uk
Free postage in the U.K., Europe; air mail at cost.

Copyright © 2008 by Mark Sarro
Library of Congress Control Number: 2008926491

Designed by RoS
Type set in Burton's Nightmare 2000/NewBskvll BT

ISBN: 978-0-7643-2996-8

Printed in China

Dedication

This book is dedicated to my wife, Katharine, thank you for your love and support.

Acknowledgements

Thank you to all of the members of CCPRS (Chester County Paranormal Research Society); past and present: Carol Starr, Kim Ritchie, Katharine Sarro, Isaac Davis III, Dinah Roseberry, Kyle Heller, Ken Leslie, Cindy Starr-Witman, Ruth Himes, Karen Rodemich, and Michele Rainey. Your dedication and support has been greatly appreciated. I also want to thank the other investigators who have contributed along the way: Christine Rodriguez of ECHO (East Coast Hauntings Organization), Deb Estep of CCPI (Chester County Paranormal Investigators) and Robin Van Pelt, founder of United States Ghost Chasers.

Thank you to all those who participated and contributed stories and anecdotes for this book.

A very special thanks goes to Dinah Roseberry for her continued patience and support along the way. Thank you!

Foreword

Welcome reader, I would like to invite you along as the following pages take you on a journey inside the paranormal. This book is the result of months of research, hard work, and collaboration. The process has strengthened my relationship with the author as both a friend and a colleague and that is how I came to this. What originally brought us together is a mutual interest and passion for the paranormal. It is that passion that drove me to the Chester County Paranormal Research Society (CCPRS) and it is that passion I hope to convey using this book as the medium. So when I was asked to write a foreword and help with the Introduction, I was both honored and overwhelmed. Overwhelmed by the opportunity to share with the reader some of my thoughts and ideas on a topic I love and enjoy.

This book is a labor of love, an intellectual endeavor into the paranormal. On my journey inside the paranormal, I have met some interesting people and seen some fascinating sights, but we will save them for another time. This book is not about me, it is about the brave individuals who came forth to share their experiences. It would not be possible without them. Those experiencers are the focus of this book as a collection of firsthand reports. We did not have to look all over the world to find places and individuals with stories to tell. No, we found them here in West Chester, Pennsylvania. They could be your neighbors or your co-workers, the house down the block or the public library. West Chester was chosen because it is the home for CCPRS, as well as a center point for Chester County. This book is not only to entertain, but to inform and illuminate, to bring attention to a topic that often goes unnoticed. The stories may take place in West Chester and focus on hauntings, but are representative of a larger phenomena and collection of experiences.

We chose the anecdotal story as the avenue with which to provide illumination because it allows the person to recount the experience in his or her own words. Do not dismiss these stories because they are subjective, but embrace them for that reason and use them as a rich source of insight. Please do not consider them mere commentary or social graffiti either. Look at them as gathered by investigators who embedded themselves within the society and culture within which they happened. As we mine the depths of the human psyche and experience for meaning, don't mock our methodology, but celebrate us as pioneers. Remember, in a dark room it is the first candle lit which makes the most difference.

As this book takes you on a journey inside the paranormal, you will be taking some baggage. This baggage is in the form of your preconceived notions and ideas, your fundamental worldview. You will use them to interpret, to judge; they will assist you on your journey seeking understanding. As you read the accounts, you will try to fit, squeeze, and shape them into your current understanding of the world. This process creates dissonance and some want to dismiss that which doesn't fit, while others are driven to seek an understanding. Be careful when navigating this terrain, for this might be the place of the paranormal experience.

—Isaac Davis, III
Investigator/Researcher

Contents

Introduction

I have spent most of my life having different kinds of paranormal experiences. Over the years, my interest had grown to the point where I felt it was time to put together a paranormal research team to investigate activity reported by individuals and families alike. CCPRS (Chester County Paranormal Research Society) formally came into existence in September of 2005. There had been several years of experiences that directly led to the decision to form a group at that specific time. Since then, the group has investigated many well-known and not so well-known places that have been reported to have paranormal activity.

The very nature of a paranormal experience is one that is subjective. The individual has a personal firsthand encounter with something that they believe to be paranormal in nature, whether it is a ghost or spirit, UFO, or other beyond-normal experience. The role of the group is to attempt to take these subjective experiences and collect objective physical evidence surrounding the paranormal activity in question in the attempt to prove or disprove that activity is, in fact, paranormal. With that said, I do believe that the power of the subjective experience can be life changing and can, and has, greatly affected the course that an individual will take in life. I directly attribute my own personal subjective experiences to the road that I am now on.

My earliest memory of a paranormal experience happened in a home that I lived in with my family as a young child. The house was an old Victorian-style home and had its own unique brand of charm. The house itself used to be a funeral parlor. There were concrete slabs in the basement where they would work on preparing the bodies for funerals and such. This house was not menacing or home to some spirit whose presence was troubling. In fact, it was quite the opposite. The house had a very welcoming feeling to it and whatever was in that house made its presence known, but in a way showing that it meant no harm.

The kinds of things that would happen there would be that of cabinets and doors opening and closing by themselves, footsteps being heard walking the halls and stairs, and sometimes the feeling that someone was in the room and that you were not alone. I had some of these experiences firsthand. The only negative thing to have come of my time in that home was that I started having a recurring dream that stayed with me for several years. I can still remember the dream in vivid detail and now it does not frighten me as it did when I was a child, but makes me really think of what the meaning or purpose of the dream may have been.

When I first set out to collect stories for the book I thought, "This will be easy. Everyone has a ghost story!" Boy was I wrong. I found that approaching someone cold with the premise of "Hey! I'm an author collecting ghost stories, ya got any to tell?" It even proved more difficult when the area of interest for the book specifically was located to West Chester. It was on my very first day of trying to elicit stories for my book that I had heard numerous times, "Are there enough ghost stories in West Chester to write a book?"

"Of course," I would reply, "there sure are…" and really, I am thinking… "God, I hope so!" But, I quickly realized that it was all in the approach. The stories were out there and I just had to make it so that they would eventually come to me.

The stories in this book come from various people and deal with diverse locations within West Chester and the immediate surrounding area. Some people have chosen not to be mentioned by name or that the exact location of the incident not be mentioned. I have agreed to this so that the story could be told. I have interjected many of my own personal experiences as well as the experiences shared by my wife and members of CCPRS that involve West Chester and the surrounding area. My home in West Chester will be the subject of most of my own true accounts. It has been very active and remained an open case with CCPRS since the group's inception. I will tell the stories collected and share the experiences in a way that will stay as true to the experience as possible.

I will also explore the nature of some of these kinds of experiences and explain with some detail about the types of activity and theories regarding paranormal phenomena. There will be terminology used throughout the book and definitions are provided in the appendix that appears at the end of the book. My goal is to enlighten, entertain, and even educate the reader to the kinds of paranormal activity that seems to be taking place all around us in our everyday lives.

Enjoy!

—Mark Sarro
Investigator, Researcher
CCPRS

Section 1

DESIGNER SHOE WAREHOUSE®

DSW

Visit dsw.com for COMP VALUE pricing details
and our return and exchange policies.

DESIGNER SHOE WAREHOUSE®

DSW

Visit dsw.com for COMP VALUE pricing details
and our return and exchange policies.

DESIGNER SHOE WAREHOUSE®

DSW

Visit dsw.com for COMP VALUE pricing details
and our return and exchange policies.

DESIGNER SHOE WAREHOUSE®

DSW

Visit dsw.com for COMP VALUE pricing details
and our return and exchange policies.

DSW.

Designer shoes. Warehouse prices.

29355 - DSW DSW

ORDER CONFIRMATION

TOTAL   109.99

ORDER NUMBER   7771014639923
ORDER DATE   09/05/22
SHIP TO ZIP: 19530

09/05/22   12:25 PM

The Residual Haunting

I have often had to describe this type of haunting as a video/audio loop. It is the same series of events that will repeat over and over again. The Residual Haunting is just that, it is a remnant or imprint of an energy of something, someone, or event that had happened at a particular place in the past. Residual Hauntings are among the most common types of hauntings experienced at any given location. The location of the building, property, and its attributes can greatly affect and influence the strength and longevity of the Residual Haunting that is being experienced. Oftentimes, a full-body apparition may be seen or the sounds of its presence (i.e., footsteps, etc.) and in some cases, physical contact (sense of being touched, pushed or poked).

A tragic event doesn't have to take place to cause a residual haunting. It is an imprint, if an action is repeated many times in some form of pattern or routine, eventually the action is imprinted onto an area. The individual who then comes in contact with it will experience it in a way that can be perceived as being outside the mind and taking on a physical manifestation. Unfortunately, though, in some cases of Residual Haunting, there are severely tragic events that have taken place and it has greatly affected the intensity of the residual activity that is happening.

A Residual Haunting can not interact with the living; it does not take notice of you as you take notice of it. It will continue to do what it does, over and over again, until it burns itself out. In some cases of Residual Haunting, the activity may only take place on the anniversary that the original event took place.

The Ground Round Restaurant

The building that once held the Ground Round restaurant stands all alone on West Chester Pike (Route 3) just outside of West Chester in West Goshen Township. The restaurant is the site of a tragic incident where a little girl choked to death. The incident supposedly happened while under different ownership and before the restaurant closed.

There have been reports of lights turning on and off and items being moved about the restaurant. Unfortunately, the restaurant has been vacant now for more than several years and a thorough investigation of the activity can not be completed. I have been researching the history of this event and have found little evidence to back up the claim that, in fact, a little girl did choke and die at the restaurant.

It is my hopes that in writing about this reported incident that someone may come forward with more information. Although I can not verify that it did happen, there have been reports of a lone girl standing out in front of the restaurant.

The Little Girl

It was early in the evening on a mid-summers night when I was driving home from work. I was several miles from home and traveling west on West Chester Pike towards West Chester. Slowly the Ground Round Restaurant was coming into view on the right-hand side and there I saw, standing all alone in the parking lot in front of the restaurant, a little girl. She couldn't have been more then eight years old, and she just stood there staring blankly out at the traffic going by.

The Ground Round Restaurant sits back off
Route 3, West Chester Pike. The spirit of
a little girl is often seen on the grounds of
the restaurant.

For some reason I felt compelled to pull into the parking lot to see if this little girl was lost or needed help. In the moment that I pulled into the parking lot, the little girl disappeared right before my eyes. I knew then that what I saw was something strange. I couldn't be sure if I hallucinated seeing the little girl, or if, in fact, that I did see her... but I know that I had.

—Anonymous

A Day at CCHS—Chester County Historical Society

In the final weeks of the 2006 CCPRS season, I had several investigators from another group, ECHO (East Coast Hauntings Organization) in town from North Carolina for a weekend investigation at Eastern State Penitentiary (ESP) in Philadelphia. (The details of this exciting investigation can be found in *Philadelphia Haunts* by Katharine Sarro, by my wife and co-founding member of CCPRS.) My wife and I wanted to show our visiting investigators as many places in and around the area as possible while they were in town.

We had decided that on the day of the ESP investigation that we would take them to the Chester County Historical Society Museum and Library located on North High Street (just past Chestnut Street). Chris, (the founding member of ECHO) was complaining about the lack of information available on the history of places and the area where she lived. She was curious to see the CCHS Library and I thought that a visit to the museum would be informative and educational as well.

The Chester County Historical Society on
North High Street in downtown West Chester.

This building is part of the Historical Society Museum that stands to the left of main building.

In my research over the past few months, I had found several accounts about the CCHS building having paranormal goings-on and that there was some activity in the museum. The interesting thing is that I could not find any paranormal groups that had investigated it and there wasn't much of anything in any books on the related subject. I had asked several times during my visit to the library for research if anyone had ever experienced anything strange or unusual, but no one would talk about it or had any experience that they wanted to share. On the day of the visit to the museum, I didn't realize that I was about to witness firsthand that there was something present in the museum. The following is the account of our trip to the museum as told by Christine, the founding member of East Coast Hauntings Organization.

Introduction to East Coast Hauntings Organization (ECHO) and Christine Rodriguez

I am the director of East Coast Hauntings Organization, currently located in Washington, North Carolina. I am also a psychologist and a clairsentient (sensory intuitive), able to feel certain energies which may be related to paranormal anomalies, including possible spirit energies. My studies include scientific research on survival of consciousness after death theories and my abilities aid greatly in locating potential paranormal hot spots for further documentation. Jack is clairvoyant. He sees images of places and people from the past as well as current entities. Intuitive abilities are just another tool used along with tape recorders, cameras, thermometers, etc. for inquiry into this, as yet, very new field of discovery among academics and scientists.

—Christine Rodriguez
East Coast Hauntings Organization (ECHO)
www.ghostecho.com

Chester County Historical Society Museum

The walkthrough of the Chester County Historical Society Museum on 225 North High Street was very interesting. There are a phenomenal number of wonderful historical antiques and objects within these walls. All are very professionally displayed and excellently maintained by the Chester County Historical Society.

I felt a brief female energy on the stairs leading up from the ground floor and a very strong male energy in the large museum room containing the grandfather clocks. Areas which I considered hot spots in this upper room included the rear wall displaying two of the largest Queen Anne clocks, the potato trenching machine with a stack of old doors and windows/arches beside it, the glass display with women's hats inside, a lounging couch inside a period-room display, and the wall aisle between the H. Pippin wood carvings and a display case with a sword and other paraphernalia.

There was definitely an attraction for me to the last Queen Anne Walnut Tall Case Clock made by Isaac Thomas. My impression was that someone who owned it constantly wound it. The residual energy surrounding the clock felt female and pleasant to me. While discussing the clock with the others in the group, a strong male energy became present next to me. This was what I consider to be interactive or sentient paranormal energy. The energy lingered for about a minute, than dissipated.

By far, the most intriguing event in the museum was the energy surrounding the H. Pippin carvings to the right of the clock area. On the wall there were two wood panels called *Bear Hunt I and II* done in 1930. These are completed with oil on pine board. As soon as I walked up to the wood pictures, a sense of vertigo came over me. I quickly left the area and asked Katharine to go back there and tell me what she thought. She lingered there a bit while I walked around some more of the room. When I returned to speak with her, she said that she felt dizzy and head-achy. She confirmed what I felt without me prompting her with information.

I studied the pine boards closer and got the impression that energy was coming from either the wood used to make the carvings or from an emotional essence of the artist who created the images. The energy surrounding these carvings was intense, focused, and indicative to me of a medical problem of some sort. I told Mark and Katharine to try and find out if the artist had a long-term illness.

Mark and Jack also came over to the carvings and felt dizzy.

They indicated to me that the display case beside the carvings held Civil War artifacts, including a sword. Jack felt strongly that the sword was the focal point of the energy, but my feeling was that it was not the display case item but the Pippin boards that generated the physical reactions we were having.

There is also an oil on canvas painting by Pippin called *Mr. Prejudice* to the left of the pine boards. This painting had no energy associated with it that I could feel.

During this second time in front of the Pippin boards, the same active male energy I felt near the clocks came over to me very strongly. I don't think this was in any way attached to the carvings, but a different soul who wanders the museum. Perhaps, this male entity is associated with the sword Jack related to.

I want to add that my feelings around the potato trencher were one that an injury may have occurred with the machine some time in its history of use. The doors and window frames beside the machine may have also generated their own hotspot aura as things such as doorknobs and portals, especially old wooden ones, are constantly used and seem to hold emotional energies.

Jack was also attracted to the case with woman's hats, particularly a white broad-rimmed bonnet with a blue ribbon on it. I did not know about this until after I had seen the display case and moved on. I also felt the hats were a hotspot of residual energy. Jack and I did discuss the potato trencher area much later after we had both seen it separately. It was a hotspot for him as well, but he was drawn to the doors and windows rather than the trencher.

It was interesting to note that as we entered this museum room via stairs, that Mark remarked about the large bronze memorial plaque on the wall above an antique writing desk to me. Then upon leaving to go back up the stairs, he again pointed to it and remarked that he liked it. I had been drawn to the desk upon entering myself. That area could also be a spot where something active lingers, perhaps the male energy I felt twice in the museum room just beyond.

Update

In the gift shop, I bought a thin book about Horace Pippin, a Chester County-born artist who lived from 1888-1946. Pippin acquired fame as one of the foremost American folk artists of the Twentieth Century. This black painter becomes known for his scenes which recalled families, heroes, history, and memories of his life.

His life included many personal tragedies as well. His mother fell ill when he just a teen; he served in the Army during WW II and was gravely injured in France by a sniper. His wife Jennie lost her sanity and was committed to an institution in 1946 after he had found popularity and became extremely distanced from his home life on West Gay Street. He died in July 1946—his wife two weeks later.

I was most interested in reading about Pippin's physical illness which haunted him throughout his life. His sniper injury prohibited him from performing his old job at the American Brakeshoe Company after his honorable discharge from the Army in 1919. He never regained full use of his right arm. After the Army, he lived on a $22.50 a month disability pension while Jennie took in laundry. It was then that Pippin began filling his hours with primitive art materials and burning pictures into wood panels with an iron poker.

During this period of physical recovery, Pippin held the poker against his knee and moved the wood panel with his left hand. His damaged right arm was so weak that the work was slow and painstaking. By 1927, Pippin moved on to using oils or canvas as well. The museum panels were completed in 1930 during his 1920s and 1930s period when he was exorcizing the pain and trauma of his war experiences.

Pippin once told a friend that "he came to paint because of loneliness." Pippin also believed that his paintings were as accurate as photographs. He painted a subject exactly as he remembered it, claiming that pictures just came to his mind and he told his heart to go ahead. Often described as a large, compelling man whose face continually drew the eye, Pippin may very well have left something behind in these pine board paintings.

Gunshots and Soldiers

On September 15, 1777, wounded American troops were escorted into West Chester by their British captors after the battle of the Brandywine. The troops were brought to the Turks Head Tavern. The tavern had been turned into a make-shift hospital to take care of the American wounded. The following day, more British troops arrived in pursuit of the other fleeing American troops. A small skirmish erupted and on the sixteenth and seventeenth of September and West Chester had the Revolutionary War brought to their front door.

The troops that had died as a result of the skirmish were buried in a schoolyard that was across from the Turks Head Tavern and it is believed to be where the Municipal building now stands at the corner of Market and High Streets in the heart of West Chester. On the anniversary of this event, if you stand on the corner of High and Market Streets, you may just hear the gunshots and cries of the soldiers past.

The intersection of Market Street and High
Street in the heart of West Chester.

The area where the Turk's Head Tavern and Inn once stood, now a restaurant named Barnaby's stands.

The Courthouse on the
Northwest corner of Market
and High Street.

A Field of Screams

I had the pleasure of meeting Robert Hensen, a radio DJ for WCOJ. I had been invited onto his program to talk about CCPRS and the recent investigation at the Phoenixville Library that had attracted some media attention because of the "book flying" video (See a detailed account of that investigation in *Ghosts of Valley Forge and Phoenixville* by D. P. Roseberry). It was off air when Robert and I were talking that he told me of a story from his youth.

He was playing with friends in a field near where Rosedale Avenue and Route 52 meet, just on the edge of the borough. They were playing when, in the distance across the field, a tall shadow appeared before them; they watched as the shadowy figure remained still. It was in the middle of the day when this happened and it struck all of them quite odd.

The shadow began to move towards them and this caused a panic amongst him and his friends. They immediately began to flee from the scene, but as they did so, they saw the shadow move closer and then vanish right before their eyes.

The corner of Rosedale Avenue and Route 52.

Footsteps on the Stairs

I had gotten up, showered, and was brushing my teeth when it happened. The sounds of heavy footsteps were heard coming up the stairs. They stomped down the hallway past the bedroom towards the back of the house and then back up the hallway, coming to rest outside the bathroom door. I was thinking at the time that it was my wife and she was in need of the bathroom and was waiting for me to finish. I opened the door and there was no one there. I went into the bedroom to find my wife fast asleep and the house was eerily quiet.

The sounds of someone walking about the upstairs have become more frequent and seem to be centralized to the hallway at the back of the house and the stairs of this West Chester home. It has become a regular instance for my wife or I to be home alone and hear the footsteps to think that other of us was home or just returned home and of course that always turned out to be not the case.

Right: The stairs at the house on Darlington Street. On the landing, several CCPRS investigators have had experiences with the spirits of the house.

The Office

From Carol Starr, CCPRS Investigator:

About twelve years ago, I was working late one evening in an office located in West Goshen Township, Chester County, Pennsylvania. There are always noises and sounds in an office late at night—things turning on and off, pipes, etc. This one evening, I was working in my office and I heard some noises near the front door. I have a glass wall facing out that way, so I could see that no one had entered the building, plus I would have heard the locks opening in both sets of doors.

I sat there for awhile, continuing my paperwork, when I heard someone call my name out loud. I got up and walked out into the office area and called out, "Who's there?" I walked around the office and went into the back rooms. The office is all on one floor with no basement or upstairs, so it only takes a minute to check everywhere. No one was around at all. I got the chills and felt my hair standing on end, so I quickly closed up my work and went home.

A few months after my experience, I was talking with my old boss, Mr. Lucas. He had been the first mayor of West Chester (then called Burgess) from 1958 until 1966 and was an incredible source of knowledge and information about the area. I told him about my experience in the office and he chuckled! He said that he wasn't surprised that there were things going on that couldn't be explained. He told me that "in the old days," when the town was called Turks Head, there were hangings done right down the road from where the office stands and that the area around the office was a burial ground for the executed people.

I'm still working in the same office and every now and then, I'll hear a noise or a sound I can't explain. My old boss has since passed away. There are so many things I would have liked to have learned from him about the history of this town I work in.

I first met Charles Lucas when I interviewed for a job with Auto Club of Chester County back in July 1977. I started work there on August 1, 1977 and worked for six years under Mr. Lucas, finding him to be a character (to say the least), and someone who had more knowledge about West Chester and its history than many people who'd lived in the area all their lives.

After six years, I transferred to the AAA building located on Paoli Pike. It was there, as you will read, that I had an experience that I could not explain. When I had the opportunity to speak with Mr. Lucas about my experience, he kind of laughed and said, "Don't you know what that whole area was?" I, of course, said no. He told me that the area forming a triangle from there moving west to where Gay and Market Streets and that this was the very placed known for the hangings back when the town was called Turk's Head.

The Gallows

The site of the old gallows mentioned in this story is at the point where Paoli Pike and Gay Street meet and where the offices for Five Star Insurance currently reside. The imprint of those who died there still lingers and is made known from time to time on the unsuspecting public who work and live in those areas.

Those that were hung at the gallows:

Hannah Miller 1805
Edward Williams 1830
Charles Bowman 1834
Jabez Boyd 1845
George Pharaoh 1851

Left: The Gallows from the parking lot where a business now stands.

The intersection of Paoli Pike and Gay Street heading onto Gay Street from Paoli Pike. This is the sight of the Gallows where several men and women have been executed.

Nields Street Railroad Crossing

It was on May 9, 1953, that West Chester had a railroad accident that was considered to be the worst in the history of the borough. A car was struck crossing the tracks at the Nields street crossing, killing all of the passengers of the car. Joseph Petrushunas, his wife Maria, their daughter, Marie, and family friend Janet Sherman were all the victims of the horrible accident. The train was said to have been traveling too fast at the time of the accident and there was nothing there to alert vehicles of an oncoming train.

It is a common belief of paranormal investigators that the sites of tragic or other traumatic events can be a very likely place to find paranormal activity, especially when the events lead to the unfortunate loss of life.

I decided to investigate the area where the accident had taken place to see if there was any residual energy as a result of the terrible accident. When someone loses their life in a sudden and tragic way, it can cause them to be confused and unsure that they have passed on. Many times these are considered "lost souls" or "trapped spirits" that, for whatever reason, are unable to pass on to the next life—they remain here amongst the living. I have had encounters with spirits that mediums and psychics have believed to be of this kind.

When I came upon the site, there was nothing unusual about the area. I had stopped to take some pictures and take a quick walk around to see if anything would happen. Unfortunately, I did not get to spend nearly as much time as I might have wanted to. Investigating this kind of area can be difficult when dealing with a road that is still used and has local traffic and residents nearby. I fully intend to

The Rail Road crossing on Nields
Street is the sight of the worst Rail
Road accident in West Chester history.

go on the next anniversary of the accident to see if in fact anything will happen. Residual Hauntings like these, or "Anniversary Hauntings" as I like to call them, are typically most active on the anniversary of the actual date that an incident occurred initially.

There are many reported cases of this type of haunting where it plays itself out, repeating the events as they happened long ago, very much like a video loop or playback, the events unfolding as they happened, but without any awareness of the present or those around them. It is an imprint made by the impact of the original event.

My wife, Katharine, revealed to me, after discussing this story, that she had been having a dream that seemed to be eerily similar to the events as told in the preceding story. She writes about the dream as follows:

> In my dream I am young, about four years old, I am riding in the backseat of a car and I am bouncing up and down. "Nooooooo, I'm so tired of the *Itsy bitsy spider*!" I stammer, but everyone in the car is still singing it, and even doing the hand movements of the spider crawling. "No, no, no, no please stop!" I keep bouncing up and down, and I start singing "Sing polly wolly doodle all the day, fare thee well, fare thee well, fare thee well my fairy fay!" The car starts to bounce along with my bouncing and the next thing I know, I look up and there is a giant locomotive right there next to the car, but it does not stop. The next thing I hear is a loud crash and instantaneously I feel crushed.
>
> "I have often woken up from this dream with a massive throbbing headache, and my whole body aches horribly."

Update

I went back to find more on the newspaper clipping that had the details of the accident to find that the young girl who died was only four years old.

Pushed From Behind

It was during one of the training investigations at the house that one of my investigators had a firsthand encounter with one of the ghosts in the house. She had just gone up the stairs when, on the landing at the top, she felt something push her from behind.

The landing at the top of the stairs and hallway just outside of the bathroom seems to be an area that has lots of activity. There is a full-length mirror that hangs on the wall in the corner of the hallway just outside of the bathroom. On numerous occasions and various investigations at the house, there has been a measurable field or energy that was recorded by various EMF detectors and a Geiger counter. The field has been the strongest directly in front of the mirror and only seems to be from floor level and about 4 to 4.5 feet high.

One of the more unusual recorded changes in energy was made with the Geiger counter. I had been using it to gather base readings on the background radiation present in the home and it was during an investigation of the house in the upstairs in this same spot in front of the mirror that the Geiger counter started showing a drop in the background radiation. It was actually draining and I recalibrated the gauge on the Geiger counter to try and measure just how much it had drained. The Geiger counter was showing a drain of -20 r/hr. It was the only time that I had seen such a drain on the Geiger counter during an investigation. It was something that I clearly won't forget and being that it happened in my own home is something that I find to be remarkable.

The Twin Tunnels of Downingtown

Traveling on Route 322 West towards Downingtown from West Chester you will come across Valley Creek Road that goes uphill on the right side of 322 heading west. This road will take you directly to the Twin Tunnels of Downingtown which will bring you to Boot Road, where by crossing Boot Road, it turns into Quarry Road. I have driven through these tunnels many times. The drive along Valley Creek Road winds up, down, and around through the woods that line the road. During the day it is a nice drive and at night, it has a certain amount of creepiness that makes it fun.

The Twin Tunnels of Downingtown seem to have a lore and urban legend all to themselves. The interesting thing about the twin tunnels is that there are actually three tunnels, but only one of them has traffic going through it. You can see the other tunnels as you approach them from either direction.

One of the legends about the tunnels is that of a man who hung himself between the tunnels, and if you drive through, stop and beep your horn, you can see him. There is also another story of a young woman who hung herself while holding a baby. Another legend tells of a body found in a suitcase inside the tunnel that was supposedly put there by a motorcycle gang that had committed the crime.

The Twin Tunnels of Downingtown from the Quarry Road
side of the Tunnels.

Valley Creek road is accessible from Route 322 heading west and will take you directly to the Twin Tunnels of
Downingtown.

The General Anthony Wayne Statue

The Residual Haunting, imprints from the past are all around us; sometimes they can be of inanimate objects that for whatever reason have attracted energies that can cause strange and unusual things to happen. West Chester is less than twenty-five minutes away from Valley Forge. The following story is an excerpt from *Ghosts of Valley Forge and Phoenixville* by D. P. Roseberry:

> General Wayne was a colorful character during the Revolutionary, his fired enthusiasm taking him into and out of trouble, it seems, throughout the Revolutionary War. Some called him quick-tempered and very self-opinionated, but he was a fighter and earned the name *Mad Anthony* for his heroic ways.
>
> Born near Philadelphia at Waynesborough in Chester County, Wayne was named after his grandfather. Having held a variety of positions in the Continental Army, he was part of General George Washington's long winter of 1777-78 at Valley Forge.
>
> His lifespan (1745-1796) is well-remembered in history, and his last days (though not at Valley Forge) are recorded by author Rupert S. Holland in *Mad Anthony,*
>
> *In November, 1796, the general and his staff of officers went aboard the sloop Detroit. All the town and all the garrison were on the wharf to bid him farewell and a mighty chorus of cheers arose as the sloop pushed off and headed south to the lake.*
>
> *Lake Eire was covered with whitecaps and the sloop made slow progress against head winds and waves that rocked her from bow to stern. The voyage had not continued long when the general began to feel his left leg growing increasingly painful. The leg was swollen, and each lurch of the ship made it ache anew. The discomfort was mounting when the sloop, after a long, stormy voyage, anchored in the bay off Presque Isle, an old fort that had been built by the French, had been held for a time by the British, and was now occupied by a few Americans.*

The General Wayne statue in Valley Forge Park. *Photo by Kim Ritchie.*

To this fort, with its crumbling walls overgrown with ivy, that watched over the lake from the southern side—where the Pennsylvania city of Erie was afterwards to rise—his aides carried the general, and they tried to make him comfortable in a bed in the main blockhouse. There was no doctor in the fortress, none in the wilderness around the lake. The commander of the post sent a messenger to Philadelphia, another to Fort Lafayette, but both those places were far distant from lonely Presque Isle.

Days passed. Gales lashed the lake and sent the spray flying above the windows of the fort. The last of November brought snow. For two weeks in December, Wayne fought the inflammation in his leg. But with no skilful surgeon at hand, he had to fight alone against that old wound, received so many years ago from the bullet of the sentry outside Lafayette's headquarters on the River James, and against the gout that had followed in the wake of the wound.

Early in the morning of December 15, 1796, the commander of the post, who was watching by Wayne's bedside, heard the general murmur: "Bury me at the foot of the flagstaff, boys."

That was the last message of Anthony Wayne. They did as he asked.

But it's what happens after General Wayne's death that is bizarre and ghostly. Ghost Investigator Carol Starr picks up the story from here. "Moving forward thirteen years to 1809, Wayne's daughter, Margaretta, was quite ill herself (she died the following year and was buried at St. David's) and made a request of her brother, Isaac, to bring their father's remains back to the family burial plot at St. David's in Radnor. No doubt expecting his father's body to be fairly decomposed after thirteen years, Isaac makes the trip in a light wagon. However, things did not turn out quite as planned. Isaac arrived at Erie and enlisted help from a doctor— and possibly several other people—in exhuming the body of Anthony. Despite the passage of thirteen years, the general's body was nearly perfectly preserved, and it was quite obvious that Isaac's small wagon would not be large enough to carry the body back to Eastern, PA. At this point, the story takes a decidedly odd twist. It is decided that only the bones would be sent back East with Isaac. This was accomplished by cutting the body of the general into pieces and literally boiling the flesh away from the bones! The question arises as to whether or not Isaac knew about the entire process or was simply

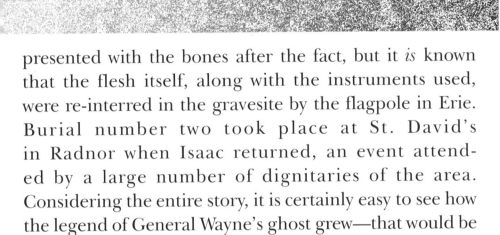

presented with the bones after the fact, but it *is* known that the flesh itself, along with the instruments used, were re-interred in the gravesite by the flagpole in Erie. Burial number two took place at St. David's in Radnor when Isaac returned, an event attended by a large number of dignitaries of the area. Considering the entire story, it is certainly easy to see how the legend of General Wayne's ghost grew—that would be one mighty confused spirit, I would think!"

Investigator Starr continued with the ghost tale. "A tour guide at Valley Forge Park shared a story of General Wayne's statue, which is located in the park. On clear nights with a full moon, the head on the statue rotates!"

Still another legend tells us that so many bones were lost along the road during the trip from Eire to Radnor—an area that encompasses much of our modern-day Route 322— that on January 1st (on Wayne's birthday), his ghost can be seen wandering along Route 322 looking for his lost bones.

Section 2

Crisis Apparitions

A crisis apparition is the spirit or ghost of someone who is still alive and appears to a loved one or family member moments before a tragic event or even their own death. It can be interpreted as an attempt to get the attention of the loved one or family member to whom it appears or simply a final chance for that person to say goodbye.

A Day to Remember

"I found myself in a strange and unusual situation on that rainy day last fall," Sara said as she shifted in the chair before me.

Sara's Story

It was a Saturday morning and I awoke with a nasty headache. It was worse then usual and I was out of anything to take. So, I knew that I would have to run to the store. Of course, the last thing I wanted to do was to have to run out to the store in the rain, especially with this pounding on the side of my head. I threw on some clothes grabbed the keys and ran out the door and into the rain. My car was just parked up the street, so I didn't bother with an umbrella or anything; I just wanted to get something to help stop the headache… It's all I was thinking about.

I went to the drugstore off of Gay Street in town. I got the pills and as I was heading out the door of the store I became overwhelmed with the smell of pipe tobacco. It was the same brand that my father smoked and it hit me in a way that caught me off guard. I turned and looked to see if anyone was nearby who had been smoking, but there was no one around. It was raining pretty heavy and I can't imagine anyone would have been standing out here in it. I really didn't think much of that incident at the time. I jumped back in the car and headed back across town towards home. I was on New Street at the corner of Miner and as I started to go through the intersection, a guy on a bicycle came out of nowhere. I had to slam on my breaks to avoid hitting him. I jerked forward, and as I sat back and looked up into the rearview mirror, I saw something that I wasn't expecting. There in the back seat on the passenger side sat my father.

The smell of tobacco again consumed me, and as I looked in shock and amazement, he reached out to me and was trying to speak but nothing could be heard. I turned in an instant to face him in the back seat and he was gone! He had disappeared in the blink of an eye. I thought I was losing it. I knew the headache was bad, but I couldn't be that bad off that I was seeing and smelling things—or could I?

I sat there for a moment trying to collect myself. I found myself thinking about how my father and I haven't spoken in a long time; we had a falling out and I just couldn't bring myself to deal with it. Of course, now I would take it all back and would have never let things happen the way they did. I sat there for a minute or two and it took a car honking from behind me to snap me out of it.

I got home several minutes later and ran into the house and straight for the kitchen to get myself a glass of water so that I could take some pills. I opened the bottle, threw back a few pills and followed it with water. I walked out of the kitchen slowly and down the hallway to the living room. I noticed that my phone was blinking and that there was a new message on my phone. I didn't notice it earlier, but then I again I didn't stop to look. I picked up the phone and dialed into my voicemail.

The message began with a long silent pause; I almost hung up the phone, but then I heard the voice speak… 'Sarah…I love you…' It was a soft and raspy voice. I had to listen to it several times, but still couldn't figure out who it was. I checked Caller ID and there had been no new calls in the last twenty-four hours and the last call I'd gotten was from a friend.

I put the phone down and proceeded to the living room and plopped down on the couch. I just wanted the headache to go away. I sat in the dark and slowly finished my glass of water. I eventually fell asleep on the couch. I often spent my Saturdays like this. These headaches were becoming all too frequent. They had intensified about a month or so ago and would come like clockwork. I am not sure how long I was asleep for, but I awoke to the sound of the phone ringing. At first I wasn't going to bother getting it—my headache was still there—but instinctually I jumped up and ran to answer the phone.

"Hello?" I said.

"Sara?" A lady's voice questioned.

"Yes," I responded.

"It's your Aunt Carla…"

"Oh, hi Aunt Carla, how are you?"

"Your father… he is really sick and in the hospital. The doctors say he could go at anytime; you need to get here…He's been asking for you and wanting you to come see him now for about a month! We have been trying to reach you, but you changed your number…" Aunt Carla stated.

"I…I didn't know… What hospital? Where is he?" I stammered.

"Chester County, come right away…" she said quickly and then hung up before I could get a chance to respond. I grabbed my keys again and rushed out the door and to the hospital.

I arrived and went to the main desk to find out what floor and room he was in. Arriving at the room, I slowly entered. The sounds of a heart monitor and other life support machines filled the room. My Aunt Carla, Uncle John, and some other members of my family were holding vigil around my father. They parted so that my father could see me.

It shocked me at first to see the state that he was in. He was pale and gaunt and looked like he had lost a lot of weight. There were numerous IVs stuck in him and he had a breathing tube coming out of his nose to supply oxygen. Very slowly he raised his head to see who it was that everyone was looking at.

He saw me and I saw him; his eyes glassed over and so did mine. I rushed to his side and took his hand in mine and looked down at him. He looked back up at me, blinked hard and then began to speak… "Sara…I love you…" In that instant he closed his eyes and the heart monitor started squealing.

His heart had stopped and the nurses and doctors came rushing in. I stepped back and everything slowed down; I felt like time was slowing down, too. The shock and realization that the voice on my voicemail from earlier that morning was my father's voice had finally hit me. I watched as they tried to revive him, but it was of no use.

He died… That day he died. I forgave him for everything he did in that moment, but he still died. My headache went away as soon as they pronounced him dead and I haven't had one since.

It's been eight months now since his death and I still remember everything from that day as if it just happened yesterday.

Sara finished her story and took a sip from her coffee. She sat there in silence for a few moments. I stopped and thought to myself that her father was reaching out to her so that he could say goodbye and move on. The headaches had intensified as her father's health became worse. The fact that the headaches stopped at the moment of her father's death seems to show that there is some sort of connection between the two.

Harry Has a Visitor

Harry never thought that there would be any reason to worry today. *Everything will go according to plan,* he thought to himself. He had just made settlement on his new house in West Chester and was eager to get the house ready to move into. It was the start of a new chapter for Harry. The divorce was final and this was the big step towards a new life. He arrived at the home and pulled into the driveway. It was bright warm sunny Saturday morning and he knew he had a full day of work ahead of him. Harry got out of his car, went to his trunk, and grabbed his tool box and other supplies he would need to get the house ready. It was minor cosmetic work that was needed and Harry was fairly certain that he could get it done over the course of a single weekend.

He stepped through the front door and into the foyer that opened up to the living room. The air was thick and heavy; he noticed it was much cooler in the house than he had expected. The weather had been fairly mild lately and Harry was sure that spring was already on its way. Harry made his way over to the thermostat and saw that the air conditioner was on. He immediately shut it off and made his way up the stairs to the master bedroom. He entered the room, set his tools down and turned on the light.

It was then that he noticed that all of the windows in the room were open. "How could that have happened?" he asked himself. "I know I shut these windows!" he mumbled. His patience was already starting to wear a little thin. His temper had always been a problem and it was a large part of the reason that his marriage had failed. His wife eventually had had enough and left him. He knew then that he had to do something about it and had begun to see a counselor to help him get a handle on it. "Breath and Relax!" he reassured himself. "No reason to get excited!" he stammered.

Harry began to spread out the drop cloth and prepared the room for painting. He realized that he had left the rollers and paint tray in the car. He quickly exited the room and down the stairs. "BRRRR!" He shivered and remarked to himself that the room was colder then before. He went over to the thermostat again and saw that the air conditioner was on and this time it was set at its maximum setting.

"What the hell is going on here?" he shouted as he smacked his fist into the wall next to the thermostat. "Okay, calm down… it's not that big a deal. It's just a bad thermostat and it's an easy fix!"

Turning the thermostat off again, Harry went out the door to his car and popped the trunk. There he found the rollers and paint tray soaked with some unknown fluid. He then found the now empty bottle of spare anti-freeze that he had been keeping in his trunk for emergencies. "How did this happen?!" He knew that it was a new unopened bottle and there was no way the cap would have just come off like it had. Harry was really starting to get agitated; he could feel his blood pressure rising. "Ahh! Now I have to go to the store and get more supplies!"

Harry went to the store again and got the supplies he needed and decided that, while he was there, he would go ahead and get a new thermostat. On his way back to the house from the store, he started to think about his ex-wife and how he really wished things could have ended better. He never meant to hurt her, he did really love her, but his temper and moodiness just was too much for her to handle.

He still remembered the day that she'd left as though it were just yesterday.

He had just come home from work and found her packing her clothes into a suitcase.

"Harry I can't take it anymore!" she yelled at him.

"What are you doing?" he shouted back.

"I'm leaving…This house isn't big enough for me, you, and your temper! Besides, my father is sick and he needs constant care, so I'm going!" she replied. She finished putting clothes into her suitcase, slammed it shut, grabbed it, and stormed past Harry, almost knocking him over. She went right for the door and never looked back.

Harry was left dumbfounded and confused. He knew that things weren't good, but he hadn't realized that it was that bad. It was only a few days later when he was served with divorce papers, and within a few weeks of that, it was all over—the divorce was final.

Looking back he couldn't believe that it all happened so quickly; from the day she left to the day he sold the house, it had only been three or four months.

Harry was quite distracted by his thoughts as he drove. He managed to get his attention back just in time to swerve from hitting the old man who was standing in the middle of the road. "HOLY CRAP!" he screamed as he turned the wheel and slammed on the brakes.

The car skidded off of the road and onto the gravel shoulder heading towards the ditch. It slid to a stop and a cloud of dust rose out from under the car. He jumped out of the car wanting to give the guy a piece of his mind… But looking back, the man was gone, nowhere to be found. He smashed his fist into the roof of his car and let out a sigh of frustration. He looked down to find that his front driver side tire was flat. The slamming on the brakes and skidding off the road was too much for it—the tire was shot. He thought that this day was supposed to be easy, but now it was turning into a big headache. This was going to be a pain, because he didn't have a working spare tire for the car. He grabbed his cell phone and called for a tow truck. It was going to be a while before the truck would get there to help him out.

Plopping down on the side of the driver side front seat, Harry sat with his legs outside of the car; he had the door open and sat facing a field with a hill that went rolling upwards to a line of trees. West Chester Pike was full of trees and fields with houses and small communities along the road, tucked off behind some trees. He knew that there was little he could do now to change the situation, so he tried to relax and just wait it out, hoping that the tow truck would get there sooner than later.

It was several hours and a couple of hundred dollars later before his car was fixed and he was able to get back to the project of working on his house, though. He finally arrived back at the house with new paint rollers and trays and a new thermostat for the heating/air conditioner unit. He grabbed the supplies and headed into the house again.

As soon as he entered the house, he was hit with a wave of heat. Immediately, he ran over to the thermostat and saw that the heat was on and was set as high as it could go. He turned it off and stopped himself from having a tantrum, feeling pushed to his limit. Harry knew that if he didn't try and calm himself down that he would end up doing something that he would regret.

"What keeps doing this?" he asked himself. This wasn't something that was mentioned as a problem when he'd looked at the house initially. But if it was the thermostat, then it wasn't really that big a deal—more of a pain in the ass then anything else.

He figured that this was as good as place as any to start with his repairs. He went over to his tool box, grabbed a screwdriver, and started to change the old thermostat to the new one. It didn't take him long and shortly, he was ready to get onto some painting that he had wanted to get to for hours.

The rest of the day seemed to go fairly uneventful; he got painting done in most of the rooms and he felt that he definitely made up for some lost time. It was getting to be early evening now and he realized that he had not really eaten anything all day. He decided to stop and go grab a bite to eat at one of the neighborhood bars.

Putting down the rollers and sealing up the paint, Harry exited the room, and in that moment, he saw movement out of the corner of his eye coming from down the hallway to his left. He turned to see what it was, but nothing was there. He swore he saw something or someone…

Harry decided to go down the hall to make sure—to check it out. Checking each room, there was no one there; the doors were left open, as he had just been in them painting. He turned again and went down the stairs to the first floor. He was about to leave for dinner, but decided to check the thermostat to make sure everything was working fine. Walked over to it, he found it to be still in the off position, just as he had left it after installing it.

"Good, it's just how it should be!" he said as he made his

way out the door.

Harry returned several hours later, but had decided that he would get a fresh start the next day. He was tired and didn't feel like doing anymore that night. He got into his car and made his way back to his old house that was full of bad memories. He took comfort in the fact that this would probably be the last night he would be staying there. He planned on moving his bed and some other things over to the new house the following day.

Harry arrived home and entered the house. It was a mess because of all the packed boxes and loose things still about from getting ready to move. He was amazed by how much junk he actually owned, but didn't care. He still had a few weeks to be totally out and he figured that he would move it bit by bit.

He headed up the stairs and right to the bathroom to take a shower. At the time he didn't bother to stop and check the phone to see if there were any messages, but, in fact, the phone was flashing and giving a signal that there was a message. He just wanted to get to bed so that he could get up early enough to make up for some of the lost time from the day's flat-tire episode.

Harry got out of the shower, threw on some clothes, and climbed into bed. He laid there thinking about the day's events and started to feel ashamed by the way that he was reacting to the thermostat and other minor problems that had arisen throughout the day. He knew that he was better then that and that he should not have allowed himself to get upset over such simple things.

He then started thinking about almost hitting the old man that was out in the middle of his lane on Route 3. It was such an odd thing, one moment there was nothing there, the next the man was there, he swerved, came to a stop, and looked to see that the man was no where in sight. The road was such that there was no way that the guy could have moved along so fast that he would already be out of sight. It was definitely strange and also that, in some weird way, the old man seemed very familiar to him.

Harry was now feeling the effects of being tired and the drowsiness was starting to take hold. He was slowly beginning to drift off to sleep when at the foot of the bed he thought he saw a figure standing. It instantly woke him up; he sat up to take a better look, but no one was there. Harry lie back down again and felt a little uneasy, but in no time he started to drift off to sleep again.

"Harry…" a soft whisper called out. "Harry…" it called out again.

Harry jumped up again and was fully awake once more. He'd just heard someone call his name, but was really unsure of whether it may have been the start of a dream. Harry again, lay down but was feeling more uneasy then before. His mind was starting to come up with all kinds of strange scenarios as to what was going on, but he knew that it was just sleep getting the best of him. Then came a loud thud at the end of the bed…

"HARRY!" a voice shouted.

Harry shot up straight out of bed and sat there eyes wide and alert. He got very little sleep that night; there were no more incidents, but enough had happened to keep him lying awake in bed all night.

The clock had just turned to 6:30 as Harry rolled over to face it. He decided that he might as well get up and start the day.

Throwing on his work clothes, he started to take some boxes out to the car. He quickly realized that he was going to have to rent a truck in order to get his bed and any of the other furniture still in the house. Deciding to pack his car with as much as he could, he headed to the house to finish up what he could before going to rent a truck.

Harry was alone in all of this. He had no real friends that he could call on to help him and the only family that he had was his ailing mother who could barely stand, yet alone help move his stuff. Besides, he would never think of asking his mother to do such a thing in the first place.

It was about 7:30 in the morning when he arrived at his new home with the car packed full of stuff. He had it all planned out. "Quickly unpack the car, get in there and get the painting done, go get lunch, get the truck, pack it up, and be back here with enough time to unpack and do some more work," he thought to himself. "I am definitely not staying another night in the old house—especially after what happened last night."

Harry still wasn't sure of what happened; he convinced himself that it was nerves and the stress of the day that kept him awake all night. He felt confident that the voice he heard was nothing more then the early start of a dream as he fell asleep.

Harry unpacked the car and was relieved to find that the thermostat had not turned on or caused any more problems. It really drove him crazy when the old thermostat was acting like it was. It reminded him of his father-in-law and how he would always turn the thermostat up no matter how warm or cold it already was. The last year or so of his marriage, his father-in-law became less and less capable of taking care of himself as senility and the onset of Alzheimer's took him. He had fond memories of his father-in-law; before he became really ill, he had always treated Harry well and never gave him any grief.

Harry thought now of what his ex-wife must be going through with having to take care of her father. "I can't imagine it's gotten any better and I am sure it has only gotten worse," he thought to himself as he painted and reminisced about his father-in-law.

Fortunately for Harry, the rest of the day went without incident. He managed to get the painting done and get the truck and most of his furniture in one trip.

It was early evening now as he finished unloading the truck and began to put his bed together. He knew he was going to sleep well tonight, after a long day of work and moving with little to no sleep. By the time he finished getting the bed put together and made up, he realized just how tired he was and knew that he was going to go right to bed, not bothering with taking a shower. He planned on getting up early the next morning and going back for whatever he could at the house with the truck before he brought it back to where he'd rented it from. He quickly undressed and fell into bed.

It was no time at all before he was dozing and starting to fall into a dream. He slept pretty well through most of the night, but it was just before 5 am when he awoke to someone or something standing at the end of the bed.

"Harry..." a whispery crackled voice spoke. "Harry...I just wanted to say goodbye."

The voice spoke as Harry sat up to see that it was an old

man standing at the end of his bed. It was dark and the sound of the voice didn't really help him understand who it was. He leaned over to turn on the light by his bed and when he turned back the old man was gone. Harry didn't get to see who it was, and it all happened so quickly that he still wasn't sure that hadn't been dreaming the whole time.

Harry quickly fell back asleep and rose again a short time later to his cell phone ringing. He rolled over to the side of the bed and reached down to pick his pants up off the floor; the phone was still in his front pocket. He reached in, and by the time he answered it, the phone stopped ringing. It was an out-of-state number on his phone; he didn't recognize the number and by this time, he was a little frustrated to have been woken by it. He hit the redial to call the number right back, wanting to know who was calling him at nearly 6 am on a Sunday. A woman's voice answered the phone; she was soft spoken and broken up by the sounds of tears being held back… "Harry?" the woman asked quietly.

"Yeah, who is this?" Harry asked in low solemn tone.

"It's me, Margaret," the woman replied.

"Margaret? What is it? What's going on?" Harry asked, as he realized now that it was his ex-wife calling.

"My father is dead…He died about an hour or so ago; I tried calling you yesterday—he had slipped into a coma and the doctor said he was going to go at any moment. I thought that you would want to know, to may come see him before he died."

As she finished speaking, it suddenly struck Harry that all of the weird incidents over the last few days now made sense—or kind of made sense. It was her father all along who had been trying to say goodbye. The old man in the road, the thermostat continually being turned on, and the voice and man at the end of his bed saying, "I just wanted to say goodbye…"

The voice rang in his head. It must have been him, there didn't seem to be any other explanation.

"Harry? Are you still there?" Margaret asked.

Harry then realized that he had not responded to what she had just told him; he'd sat in silence as his thoughts put it all together as to what had been happening over the past few days. "I am very sorry Margaret. Are you going to be okay?" he asked.

"Yes, it was his time. I know he's in a better place now. He has been sick for so long," she said quietly.

"As long as your okay; that's all that matters," Harry replied.

"Thank you, Harry. I am sorry that I called and then hung up. I hadn't really noticed what time it was; I haven't really slept the past few days. You know, right before my father slipped into the coma, for a brief moment he was lucid and he called out your name," she stated.

Harry spoke to Margaret for a few more minutes, said his goodbyes, and made plans to join her later in the day after he had returned the truck and gotten the last of his things. He knew that she shouldn't be alone, and despite all that has happened between them in the last year or so, he didn't want her to have to go through it by herself.

Harry and Margaret see each other more now; the death of her father has brought them closer together. And Harry has even brought to her the idea of them getting back together. He still hasn't shared with her the experiences that he had those couple of days leading up to her father's death.

He still wasn't sure exactly what to think of all of it. He had never had any kind of experience like that before and it took him all by surprise.

Needless to say, the house has been quiet since then and he hasn't had any more visitors in the night calling out his name or turning up his thermostat.

Grandfather Visits...

I have never had an experience with a crisis apparition like those told by the individuals who have shared their experiences for my book, but I have had experiences similar to this with my own grandfather. I was only thirteen years old when my grandfather died of cancer. He was the patriarch of my mother's family and was a pillar of strength that I had always looked up to. He would come to visit us at the house at least once a week and sometimes on a daily basis.

It was routine that when he would come that I would make him hot tea with sugar and no milk. We would sit and he would ask us about how things were with school and talk about other things that were happening within our family.

I was devastated when he died, I had never lost anyone who was so close to me and never thought that it would happen so soon in my own life. I was not there the day that he died, but he was surrounded by family and loved ones. I was afraid to see him so close to death. I really didn't want to see him like that and I couldn't bear saying goodbye in that way. But looking back, if I had another chance to say goodbye, I would be there right by his side. It is one of my few regrets in life; I never really got a chance to say goodbye.

Over the years since his death, I have found that in my times of great stress or turmoil he would come and visit me in a dream. It was a strange kind of awareness, where we both knew that he wasn't supposed to be there, but for whatever reason, he was. He almost never spoke to me, but the mere sight of his presence was enough to make me feel better. I would often awake immediately and still have those feelings, as though he had just been there by my side.

My wife has said that she would often awake to see someone standing over me on my side of the bed. She described the man as wearing a flannel shirt, but she couldn't always make out the features. She had made the connection that the man was the same "red plaid" ghost that has been visiting us since we moved into the Darlington Street house in West Chester. My grandfather wore flannel shirts almost all of the time, and I started realizing that, on a few occasions, when my grandfather came to me a in a dream, that it coincided with a sighting by my wife of the man standing on my side of the bed.

My connection to my grandfather is a strong one. I still have some of his belongings and wear clothing and jackets that were once his. I think about him often and am grateful to have had someone like him to be a part of my life.

I believe that he comes to me partly because we never got a chance to say goodbye when he was still alive.

Section 3

Shadow People

What are shadow people? There are a growing number of theories coming out as to the nature of this kind of phenomena. I have begun to develop my own theory as to what this phenomena is, but for now, let's quickly take a look at some of the other theories.

There is the theory that the "shadow person" is the ephemeral body of someone who is astral projecting. A lot of these reported phenomena have happened as something that is seen from the corner of the eye at the edge of peripheral vision, while still others report seeing it straight on.

The Shadow people are different then ghosts or spirits because of their lack of definition and detail. They are by their very nature a shadow or outline of a human form. One of the common features that has been reported on these creatures is that of having glowing red eyes. This in itself can be disturbing because yet another theory portends that it is that of a demonic or subhuman nature. (Of all the experiences that I have had with this phenomena, I have never seen the glowing red eyes as reported in so many other cases.)

Are these demonic beings or are they the astral body of a traveler passing through?

Still, another theory is that these shadows are beings from another dimension. This theory holds a better chance of being true because of the hard science now being explored on the nature of dimensions above and beyond the three that we have come to love. The book *Hyperspace*, by Michio Kaku, explores the theories of quantum physics and the scientific probability of dimensions beyond our ability to perceive.

The final theory on these phenomena that I will mention is that the shadows are of an Alien nature, that they are other worldly beings masking themselves in the forms of shadows in order to conduct their experiments. In many alien abduction cases, there have been reports of beings coming through walls and doing things that are beyond the natural laws of physics.

Any of these theories have their validity, some more then others, but all are based on the experiences that seem to fit in with one or more of these ideas.

My own theory is that "shadow people" and things of this nature are an energy that has manifested itself in a way whereby its form and shape depend upon the person perceiving it. The individual greatly influences the way in which it is seen. We must remember that, despite our ability to determine an object in a certain way, there are no two perceptions alike. Our perceptions, and/or reality as we perceive it, is unique to the individual. We may both see an object and can agree that the object has the same form and appearance, but its meaning in direct relation to the individual is all its own.

Hide and Seek

I was working in my office, which is the middle bedroom on the second floor of our house in West Chester and I had decided to take a little break. I had just come from the downstairs after getting something to drink. Standing in the doorway of my office, I was half in and half out in the hallway. My wife, Kat, was in the bedroom putting away laundry while the TV was on and I had turned to talk to her when something caught the corner of my eye at the other end of the hallway.

I turned to look and it was a shadowy mass with no real form, moving quickly down the hallway from Kat's office and up towards the bathroom on the left. I quickly gave chase, following it to see where it was going and what it was doing. I chased it into the bathroom and it disappeared right before me as it passed into the wall, as if going through it to the outside. I then went for my camera and EMF meter and came back, hoping to see it again—but it did not return.

This incident in the house was not the first time that I had encountered something like this. I wouldn't say that what I saw was a person or even had the shape of a person, more or less a formless vaporous cloud of a shadow, like nature. The phenomena I experienced is part of an experience that has been reported many times from around the world and has now become a classification all its own: Shadow People.

Amongst the Trees

The sun had just begun to set over Everhart Grove, a park that lies between Price and Miner Streets and along Brandywine Street. It was along "The Soroptimist Walk," the paved path that runs east and west and is accessed from Brandywine Street where Terry had her encounter:

It was just getting dark and I was taking the dog for a quick walk through the park before I had to go to work. I had just entered the park along Brandywine on the path when I noticed that something was just off to my left on the edge of the tree line.

The trees there are not so big or close together that someone could not be seen walking among them, but this was not the case. It was a tall, slender shadow that seemed to be much taller than anyone I might have ever seen. I was struck with fear, but at the same time, was intrigued by it.

When I turned to face it straight on, I could not see it, but when facing towards the path, it would appear again at the corner of my eye in my peripheral vision. There were no features, just a shadow that was transparent and moved slow and deliberately as I moved. Obviously, I made sure that it was not my own shadow and it certainly wasn't.

The dog was preoccupied with his walk and initially took no notice of the shadow that was following me. We continued down the path and came to where the path goes to the right and over the bridge. The dog was off to my right and the shadow was off to my left. It then moved so quickly from one line of trees to the next that it was just a blur, and then from there, it had disappeared altogether. That was the first time that I had ever experienced anything like that in all the years that I have been to that park.

—Terry

Everhart Grove

100 South Brandywine Street
West Chester, Pennsylvania

Everhart Park is one of the second oldest parks in the borough. It sits on 10.2 acres of land that was originally owned by William Everhart, who named the park Everhart Grove. Through the 1840s and 50s, the park was used for political rallies and a place for abolitionists to gather, but the parks main purpose was for the community. In 1851, this was the first site for the West Chester Volunteer regiment, so the military members could stay physically fit after the Civil War.

The land was donated to the borough by Dr. Isaiah Everhart in 1905. In the early 1900s, a beautification project was started because the park had become neglected and abused. A pond was built in 1909 where the wetlands are now located and rare trees were planted. The gazebo was constructed in 1908 and still stands today.

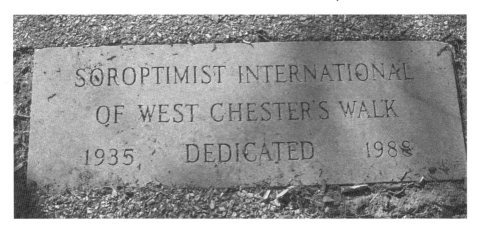

The dedication plaque that is on the walkway of the path.

The sighting of a Shadow person has been seen along this path known as Soroptimist Walk.

The plaque that is on the left stone column at the entrance to Soroptimist Walk.

Another path that cuts across the park.

Hemlock Alley (Between Barnard and Miner Streets from Everhart Grove to Church Street)

Bill had just parked his car and was taking a shortcut through Hemlock Alley on the block between New and Wayne Streets. He often walked through this alley late at night after getting home from work. He would take notice of his surroundings; he knew better then to walk through an alley or any city street without keeping awareness of where he was and who was in the area. It was something that was instilled in him growing up in Philly.

He walked slow, taking his time and not feeling rushed. It was a decent night and he liked to take his time walking to the house. He had been cooped up in a smoky bar all night and the fresh air always did him some good.

"When it happened, it was fast!" he exclaimed. "I was just about to turn up New Street when, across the street and down the alley, it moved very fast from left to right. It was dark and must have been eight feet tall or something. I never saw anything like it! It shot across the alley, and then it was gone!"

Shadow in the Doorway

From an anonymous West Chester resident:

I was coming out of the living room and was heading into the kitchen when I saw it.

It was a dark mass of a shadow, but I could see right through it. It had the shape of a human being, but was much taller and thinner than any person could be. I couldn't make out any features—it was a shadow.

I stood in the doorway between the living room and dining room and watched it as it watched me. It was like I caught it doing something it wasn't supposed to be doing; it was stopped dead in its tracks and was looking at me as I was looking at it. We stood there for what seemed like an eternity, but maybe it was only for a few minutes. It wasn't until my wife called out my name that I moved again, and it was in that quick of an instant, when I turned away, it disappeared.

I don't know what it was; it was the only time I saw it and we have never had any other experiences in the house. It was strange and it left me feeling uncertain whether I actually saw anything or whether it was my mind just playing tricks on me...

Hemlock Alley where it intersects with New Street. The sighting of a Shadow person has occurred in this area.

The Pentagram Trees

It was a warm autumn night when John and Lindsay saw the shadow person in Marshall Square Park. John recalls:

> We were walking home from dinner and it was just getting dusk as the sun went down. We were talking and not really paying too much attention to anything when Lindsay stopped in her tracks and pointed at something in the park. I looked at her and asked her what was wrong; she grabbed my arm and turned me to look.
>
> I wasn't sure what I was looking at or what she was looking at, for that matter. It was through the trees towards a small group of trees that she pointed and insisted that something was there. I asked her what it was and she said that it was something tall and dark like a person.
>
> I struggled to see it, because it was getting dark and it was much harder to see in the park. I turned back to her and asked her again when she gasped. I turned back and saw a tall, thin shadow move between the groups of trees. I didn't believe it; it had to be someone playing a joke.
>
> I made a beeline straight towards the trees where it was. I had to see better who or what it was. I remember Lindsay yelling after me, but I kept going. I stopped dead, just a few feet from the trees where it was when it moved out from behind the tree and shot straight across the park and disappeared.
>
> It must have been over seven feet tall and it was really thin. The trees where it was were smaller and would not have hidden a person as easily as it hid the shadow. I got really excited, I'd never seen anything like that before and I really didn't know what to believe.

The "Pentagram Trees" are located near the monument and is the site where another Shadow Person has been seen.

The grouping of trees grow out from the center tree and are three feet apart from each other.

A Closer Look

I visited Marshall Square Park and got as close to the exact location as possible from John's description as to where they saw the shadow person. It was much to my dismay to discover a small group of six trees that were set perfectly in the shape of a five-pointed star or pentagram.

It is an odd site and I have to wonder if they were planted intentionally in that shape or if it was merely a coincidence. I later emailed John to verify again where exactly they'd seen the shadow and it was, in fact, in the grouping of trees that I'd discovered to be in the shape of a star.

In the final weeks of preparing this book for the publisher, I went back to the park with several members of CCPRS to take a closer look at the grouping of the trees. I was immediately struck with an odd sensation as I approached them. I couldn't help thinking that it was no coincidence that the trees were grouped the way that they are.

Carol, one of my colleagues, had been taking EMF readings in the area of the trees. It was on the side of trees facing Matlack Street where there were several spikes in the meter ranging from .8 to 1.5.

This meter is made to measure A/C electromagnetic fields that are generally produced by manmade electrical devices. There are no power lines or other types of electrical devices in that specific area of the trees that would cause a spike like that, and typically, an A/C field is a constant or steady field that will increase in its measurement the closer that you are to its source. These spikes were random and inconsistent with any manmade electrical field.

I started to measure out the distance of the trees from one another, and as I began to do so, it became even stranger; the trees, for the most part, are 3 feet from each other and 2 ½ feet from the center tree on all sides. Those on the perimeter are all growing out away from center; which again struck me as a bit odd. Either way, the trees are something worth seeing for yourself.

I can only speculate at the planting of the trees in the strange pattern as intentional. It is eerily coincidental that the story of the shadow person told of this park seemed to originate from within this group of trees. This may in fact have some spiritual or ritualistic significance and the visitor of these trees should proceed with caution, because you never know what you might see or find lurking about within and amongst the Pentagram trees.

There were numerous EMF spikes within the trees during our investigation.

About Marshall Square Park
200 East Marshall Street

In March of 1841, the borough of West Chester purchased Marshall Square Park from Anthony and Adelaide Bolmer. The park was named after Humphrey Marshall in 1848. Marshall was a Botanist for the East Bradford Township.

Marshall Square Park is the oldest park in the borough and is five acres in size. The park was originally used as a water basin because the land is located at the highest elevated point of the borough. After the water basin was no longer large enough to suit the needs of the borough, the land was turned into a public park. Some of the original trees that were planted by botanists can still be found in the park today.

In July of 1886, a monument was erected in the honor of the Ninety-Seventh regiment, who had fought in the civil war. The monument stands at the highest elevated point in the West Chester borough.

Right: The Civil War monument stands on the highest elevated point in the Borough of West Chester.

Marshall Square Park, located at 200 East Marshall Street, is the oldest park in the Borough.

Section 4

Poltergeist Haunting

The word *poltergeist* comes from two German words meaning "Noisy-Spirit." I believe that the poltergeist classification of haunting has been severely misrepresented or interpreted over the years in the realm of pop-culture. A poltergeist can, in fact, be a spirit and is usually mischievous in nature. It can be very destructive and, in some cases, extremely violent, but this does not make it is evil.

A poltergeist is going to slam doors shut, open cabinets, knock things off of chairs, knock and scratch on walls, doors, and ceilings, make water appear and disappear in various ways, and sometimes can cause fires to light spontaneously. The latter is usually only apparent in the more severe of cases.

There are hundreds of documented cases that have been reported over the years. Some of the earliest investigators, such as Harry Price, have dedicated whole books to this subject. (*Poltergeist: Tales of the Supernatural* by Harry Price, Bracken Books.)

The most unusual aspect of these types of cases really didn't start to become apparent until the last thirty to forty years or so when it was realized that the activity typically centered around one person, usually a child in late adolescence or early puberty. Even more interesting is the fact that nine out of ten of those cases generally involves the activity surrounding a young female.

As more study and research was taken into these types of cases, it was soon realized that the activity was not caused by an outside force, but the person that the activity it was surrounding. The common element is that the individual is going through some form of emotional or physical trauma and stress. The activity is a result of their subconscious psychic energy building up and releasing itself in a fury of violent activity.

Another strange element in these cases is that as quickly as the activity comes on and intensifies, it also dissipates just as fast. Usually the activity can come and go in as little time as a few weeks or a few months at the most. Another interesting common element is that when the individual who is causing the activity seeks some form of counseling or other type of help, the activity will stop almost immediately and not return.

Stories about this type of activity were not as easy to come by, because in most cases, the person experiencing the activity is not fully aware that they themselves are causing it—it is perceived as some outside force. I was fortunate enough to be involved with a case in West Chester where poltergeist activity was present. The following is a retelling of the events of that case and how it was that CCPRS and I became involved.

Roommates

"It kept me up all night again!" Maria said to her roommate Vicki.

Vicki looks at Maria not sure of what to say. "What happened?" she asked hesitantly.

"The bed; it kept shaking, like someone was beating on it!" Maria exclaimed, but in a quiet voice. Maria feared that her other roommates would hear her; she knew that they already thought that there was something wrong with her. She was the newest of the five roommates and had only been living in the house for a few months. But she knew Vicki was different because they shared the same floor and that Vicki, in her own way, had had some experiences too. She would understand what it was that she was going through.

"I don't know what to tell you. Are you sure it wasn't a dream?" Vicki asked.

"NO! It wasn't!" Maria stammered with defiance.

"I'm sorry, but I just don't understand!" Vicki got up from the chair at Maria's desk and walked out of the room.

Maria, upset, fell back to her bed and began to cry. "I just don't understand it, either! Why is this happening? What does IT want?" she asked herself.

It seemed as though no sooner had she moved into the house, that things had started to happen. It was little things at first, a knock on the wall or a scratch and tapping sound on the window, and then over the course of a few weeks the sounds were coming from inside her room. Things would get knocked off of her desk, and sometimes, when sitting at her desk working on her computer, it would feel like someone was standing behind her and it would then grab the chair and give it a quick shake.

Maria sat up from the bed and wiped the tears from her face with her sleeve. "I don't have time for this! I have a paper due tomorrow and I still have more then half of it to do!" she thought to herself.

She felt fortunate enough not to be so far away from home and thought of her family who only lived an hour or so outside of West Chester.

She enjoyed living in the small town of West Chester—everything was so close and the campus was in walking distance of where she lived. She'd found love, or at least she thought she had, a nice guy who seemed to take care of her and be there when she really needed him.

But lately it has been difficult confiding in him, because nothing ever happened when he stayed over; it was always when she was alone in her room or in the house. That was something that frustrated her more then anything about the whole situation. It really made it hard for her anyone to believe her, because no one else really shared the experiences the way that she did.

Over the course of the next few months things remained about the same: Like clockwork, the bed would start to shake and vibrate and keep her awake. At this point, though, she felt that at least her roommates would understand better now, considering that the roommate who had the room right below her had experienced it, too.

Vicki and her also shared an experience when they were both in their rooms working at their desks as something came up from behind her and shook her chair, making her feel like a surge of electricity had passed through her. Within seconds, Vicki experienced the same thing.

Maria had also confided in her boyfriend more, and even though he hadn't witnessed anything firsthand, he understood the situation and wanted to make sure that she was okay. Unfortunately, with both their work and school schedules, they didn't get to spend a whole lot of time together; he was only able to spend a couple of nights a week at the house with her. The rest of the week she was be on her own to deal with whatever it was that was shaking her bed on an almost nightly schedule. It unnerved her.

Maria knew that something had to be done. It was a quiet Saturday morning when she was sitting at her computer and started to browse the Internet. She started searching for paranormal-related sites and hoped to maybe even find some local ghost hunters who she could reach out to for some help. There it was, a group located in her own backyard… "Chester County Paranormal Research Society," she read to herself. Here might be someone who hopefully would help her find some answers as to why things were happening in the house. It was almost instantly that she decided to send an email to the address that was listed on the Web site. She was curious and was compelled to find answers to all that had been happening.

This is when CCPRS became involved. Over a few weeks, I exchanged several emails and had a phone interview with Maria. I scheduled a time for when myself and several of my investigators could come to the house to conduct a formal interview and preliminary investigation. I invited Deb Estep, investigator and founder of CCPI (Chester County Paranormal Investigators) to join us for the meeting. I'd met Deb online and had emailed back and forth and spoke to her on the phone on one occasion. She taught night school classes at Chester County Night School on various topics related to the paranormal. (The school and contact information is located in the resources section at the end of this book.)

It was a Tuesday night when Deb, Tony, Katharine, and I went to Maria's house to meet with her and her roommate to discuss the events and incidents that she had encountered over the past few months.

The house was located in the part of town once known as Riggtown; it sat on a small side street just off of Matlack. We arrived at the home and stepped up onto the front porch. Maria and Vicki greeted us at the door and brought us into the living room where we would sit to talk about their experiences. The house was a row home, typical of that part of town—three story, five bedrooms with an unfinished basement, and a small yard in the back. The front door was on the left side of the house on a common wall with the home next door that also shared the porch with a divider between the two.

Upon entering the house, it opened up to a hallway with the stairs going up to the second floor straight ahead and a doorway to the right that went into the living room, with the kitchen at the back of the house. I sat on the couch next to Maria and Vicki, while Deb sat back in the corner, next to the couch with Katharine and Tony sitting on the love seat across from the sofa.

I started the tape recorder and began with the formal line of questions. I had made it clear to the others with me that night that I wanted them to sit and observe—to try to get an overall sense of the situation. Deb sat in an almost meditative state, trying to calm and quiet herself and tune into the environment about her. (I was intrigued by her methods as they were a variation off the more scientific approach that my group was taking at that time.)

Maria began to tell us in great detail of the events that had happened in the home since she had moved in. As Maria and Vicki were answering our questions, Deb and Katharine had taken notice of something in the corner of the room, in the doorway at the kitchen. Neither one of them spoke of it at the time, but I picked up on it, too, and noticed as they took mental notes of what it was that they felt was nearby.

Deb would write in her report about the interview:

> "During the interview, in the "sitting" room on the first floor, I became aware of an active energy that approached from the kitchen. I perceived the energy as male and would characterize the attitude of this individual as curious about who we were and what was going on in the room. The presence remained with us in the room for quite awhile. I later found out that Katherine had also become aware of a presence in the room. My feeling is that this energy is male."

Katharine would write about the same experience:

> "During our interview with Maria and Vicki, I sat on a sofa near the entrance to the kitchen. All throughout the interview I got chills and I felt like someone was standing next to me. The feeling I had was as if "someone" was as curious about us, as we are about them."

Upon completion of the interview, we had decided to conduct a walk through of the house with some of our hand-held equipment. I was armed with a Cell-Sensor EMF meter and we began making a sweep of the first floor. Katharine had her camera and the six of us started by entering the basement. I wanted to see the foundation of the house to find out if there were any tell-tale signs of mold or electrical wiring problems. While we were in the basement, Katharine and Deb had an experience that they both wrote about in their follow up reports.

Katharine wrote:

"When we ventured in the basement, it felt the same as my own basement at home. It was a bit creepy, but not too bad. There is a back room to the basement, and I thought I heard someone say 'no, but I meant to,' so I went in, but no one was there. I took a lot of photos in one corner that all came out blurry, as if something was moving in that corner."

Deb also wrote:

"During our walk-thru of the basement, Katherine and I were in the smaller back room at the same time. I heard a voice that I first thought was Katherine talking to herself. I asked her if she had made a comment and she indicated that she had not. I continued to hear the voice which was joined by others in conversation. The quality was distinctly female but too low to make out any words. Vicki, Maria, Mark, and Tony were in the other room and their voices were distinct and separate from this "murmured" conversation."

We had finished our tour of the basement; Maria and Vicki had reported that there hasn't been any activity there, but also mentioned that they made it a point to not go into the basement whenever possible. The overall feeling to them was that it did not make them feel comfortable.

The basement revealed just how old the house really was. It had large stone foundations and a wall with a doorway the divided the basement off from the back of the house. (This is where Katharine and Deb experienced the voices and murmured conversation.) We moved back upstairs and continued our tour of the first floor.

Katharine, Deb, and I proceeded into the kitchen where immediately the EMF meter began to go off. My instinct was to first look for any artificial electro-magnetic fields that might cause the meter to register.

In a kitchen, you'd expect to find heavy appliances that can give off higher readings and affect the overall level of the room. In this case, the readings were coming from the center of the room, and as I moved closer towards the refrigerator, the meter was not affected.

Tony had gone with the girls upstairs to see where some of the activity was taking place. I made a slow left-to-right sweeping motion with the EMF meter and crossed right through a cold spot that shot a jolt up my right arm. It hung there in mid air and seemed to be stationary.

I turned and looked at Deb, and as I did so, I knew that I had just felt something. Just as quickly as it was there, it was gone, and when I passed across the same space again with the EMF meter the cold spot had disappeared. I looked to see if a draft had been present, crossing the room from the doorway, but none was there. It was my first real sense that there was something there in the house.

Deb wrote about the experience in the kitchen:

"During our walk-through, I obtained some EMF meter readings that were indicative of energy fields (off-the-scale readings) in the kitchen, especially along the wall separating the kitchen from the sitting room where a large free-standing cupboard is located. More similar meter readings were obtained in other parts of the kitchen."

Katharine would also write:

"When we began to walk through the house I felt like there was energy located within the kitchen. The meters were going off and there were some cold spots. I thought it was interesting to find a photo that Maria had displayed on her computer screen that was taken in the kitchen—a bright white spot which could be an orb is right next to her. While in her room, I got the feeling that there was an energy that truly cares about Maria, like a father might feel for his daughter, as if he wants to protect her from something."

Kat, Deb, and I slowly made our way up the stairs and rejoined Tony who was talking to the girls in Vicki's bedroom on the third floor. Tony was asking them follow-up questions of his own, as he was trying to gain a better understanding of the types of experiences that they were having.

Tony wrote:

"I have no doubts of the girls' sincerity regarding their experiences, however I make an argument for the house being congested rather than haunted. Important note: While alone with M and V on the second floor, I asked a series of questions about their sleeping habits. M stated she does not remember her dreams often and not for many years. I also asked if either of them have experienced sleep paralysis. V has; M was unfamiliar."

I asked Vicki to retell her story and to show me how some of the activity had taken place in her room, including what she was doing at the time. She retold the experience of working at her desk and having the sudden sensation of something passing through her and shaking her chair, while mere seconds later, Maria had experienced the very same thing.

I had been monitoring the EMF readings in Vicki's room and had not measured anything that was out of the ordinary. There were a usual amount of fields generated from the computer that was in her room. Vicki had only some very minor experiences as opposed to what Maria had been encountering on an almost nightly basis.

We eventually all ended up in Maria's room. Maria was explaining the nature of the activity that she had experienced when I began to pick up an anomalous field with the EMF meter that seemed to be stationed over the center of her bed. There were no light fixtures or any other electrical outlet or device that was in the direct vicinity that would be causing the meter to have the readings that it did. I brought the meter to a stationary position over the bed where the readings were the strongest, and as I did so, the readings dropped. As I moved to try and pick it up again, the position of the higher readings changed. It was if the field was moving and I was tracking its movements by the strength of the fields that the meter was reading. It was moving across the bed, then across the room and over by the window. I did not feel any cold spots as I had previously felt in the kitchen. It was curious and everyone in the room had been witnessing what was transpiring with the energy field I was tracking across the room.

I did not initially jump to any conclusions; I had to make sure of what it was that I was measuring—whether it was an artificial field or something that was truly anomalous. Maria became a bit unsettled as we tried to determine the cause of the field and its unusual readings and movements. She had remarked that she had felt something was in the room with us, but could not really specify as to what or who it was. Again like before, the field suddenly disappeared and the EMF meter no longer picked up the readings as it had before.

Deb writes:

"After spending some time on the second floor in the rooms where the girls sleep, I feel there is a male presence who visits this area. My initial impressions are that this individual is not "young" (their own age) but older (more middle aged). I cannot say at this time whether this is the same energy as I encountered on the first floor, but it might be. The girls have indicated that the energy they encounter in their rooms is male. I have the impression that the older male energy is more protective. Perhaps there is a second male present on the second floor."

We concluded our walk through of the house. It was now later in the evening, but we did not want to do anymore then we had set out to do that night. Our plan would be to come back and complete a thorough investigation of the house at a later date. We needed time to go over the interview and our initial thoughts and experiences during the walk through.

Here are Deb's final thoughts on the events that took place that evening:

"It must be taken into consideration that the house is currently occupied by five young ladies. When I first entered the house, the energetic atmosphere was very evident to me. I would wonder how much of that energy belongs to the girls and if their combined energies are providing the conditions for the presence/manifestations of phenomena they are reporting. However, the house (the physical structure, as well as the atmosphere within the structure) seemed to relax after a bit. I would describe the house as "holding it's breath." I felt as though whatever energy was present was waiting to see what the "guests" were going to do and seemed aware of why we were there.

"I think it is significant that Vicki goes with her friend to visit and pray at a cathedral for her friend's brother who has died. I would like more information on this. She also shared an incident from her teens regarding seeing a woman die in a skiing accident in which she was involved. I would like to ask more about this incident. Maria might be the catalyst for the activity, but Vicki might be the person for whom the contact is important."

It was that very next morning that I received an email from Maria:

"Hey Mark,

I'm writing b/c I woke up about an hour and a half ago from the most vivid dream you could ever imagine—and coming from someone who has never remembered a dream in my life ever, it was definitely something else. It started with a male laying on top of me (I always sleep on my stomach) and I remember turning my neck around to try and see who this person was—he was definitely a male, I would guess in his mid to late thirties and I remember so clearly what he said—'This will be the last time I'm doing this.' I know it sounds corny, but I can still hear his voice in my head. I remember that I was trying to scream the whole time, but nothing was coming out...I do remember that I was trying to scream, "Mom." When I finally came totally out of the dream, there was such pressure on my back that I thought that Stiles (the cat) was sleeping half on my back half on my bed, but when I felt for him, he wasn't there. I don't know if this helps with anything, but it definitely caught me by surprise and seemed more vivid than a dream is supposed to be.

Thank you so much for being understanding about this. Sometimes I feel that this is a little more than I can handle— maybe because it's so unknown to me, but like you said, I'll try and lean on my faith and keep telling myself it's nothing to fear."

Unfortunately, the later investigation would never take place. The investigation had been scheduled for several weeks later and it was to take place on a Saturday night. Maria had made plans for her and Vicki to be there, but for her other roommates to *not* be present that night. It came down to the day of the investigation and to literally a few hours before when I had received a panicked phone call from Maria. She had come home from work to find that there was a keg of beer in her kitchen and that her other roommates had decided at last minute that they were going to throw a party. Maria was quite upset at the lack of consideration that her roommates had shown her.

I made another attempt to schedule the investigation, but it was all for not. I let some time pass since the failed attempt to investigate the home. I left it with Maria—that she would contact us when she thought it would be a good time to schedule the investigation. More time would pass before I would finally hear from her.

She sent me an email stating that she had moved out of the house. The extreme lack of consideration that her roommates showed her on the night of the original investigation had been the catalyst for the realization about the treatment she had received from them. She was happy to report that the activity had stopped, and that whatever it was did not follow her to her new home.

I had officially closed the case and left it that if she ever needed anything or experienced anything else that she contact us immediately.

So, what was the significance of the dream? Who was the man who came to her on that night? Roommates so often share food or other household items, but rarely do they share a ghost!

Afterwards

There was a variety of contributing factors that seemed to be causing the events that took place in the house. The core of the activity was directly surrounding Maria. The built-up tension and feelings that she had relating to her roommates played a significant part in the way that Maria perceived what it was that she was experiencing. She never had a single experience when her boyfriend stayed over at the house and only one other roommate, besides Vicki, had ever experienced anything in the house—which happened to be the sounds of Maria's bed moving across the floor as heard by the roommate who lived on the floor below.

There was definitely some other presence in the house, but it did not seem to be the direct cause of the types of disturbances that Maria had been experiencing. The tapping and pounding on the bed when she would try to sleep is a strong indication that she may, in fact, be the one causing the activity to happen. It was outwardly manifested by the stress and tension that she felt as a result of the other roommates in the house.

When she moved out, the feelings were gone and the disturbances stopped. Vicki reported no further activity in the house once Maria had moved out.

The complete report, string of emails and messages that transpired back and forth between Maria and the group is available on the CCPRS Web site for review at: www.chestercountyprs.com\mariacase.htm

Section 5

The House on Darlington Street

I would have to say that the experiences that my wife and I started having shortly after moving into our home in West Chester greatly contributed to the timing of starting a formal paranormal research group. The house became the group's first formal investigation and, over the course of the next year or so, it would be investigated numerous times and used as a training ground for some of the group's earlier members. In retrospect, investigating one's own home is probably not the wisest decision, but I felt that it was a worthwhile because we would have a better chance of capturing evidence in a place that we could investigate at will over a longer period of time.

The house itself was built in the 1860s and is a modest three-bedroom row home in heart of the downtown area. The house is full of its quirks with original interior door latches and knobs and closets that are literally six to ten inches deep! Let me take you now and a quick tour of the house.

We enter the house after going up several outside steps; through the door there is a hallway that leads to the bottom of the stairs. There is a door to the left that goes into the front room of the house and then an opening to the middle room. We never use the door that is on the left because there is a set of double doors we leave open that is accessible through the middle room. The front room has become our living and TV room and the middle room a sitting and reading room.

Continuing towards the back of the house is the dining room and at the back is the kitchen, which is an addition to the house and not original to the time it was built. The basement door is also located in the dining room. There is a back door that exits in the kitchen going out into a small fenced in yard. The kitchen is small, but has a surprising amount of cabinet space. The ceilings are twelve feet high in the dining room, middle, and front room. There is a closet that is built out into the room in the middle room that has a shelf/ledge on top. Going up the stairs and straight to the back of the house is Kat's office, to the left of the bathroom and back down the hall towards the front of the house is my office on the right (middle room) and our bedroom is located at the front of the house. My office and the bedroom is also joined by a door that is in the corner of the room near our closet. There is a closet in the hallway outside the door which is where the attic crawl space is accessed. This is the biggest closet in the house and where we keep the bulk of our linens and clothing.

The hard wood floors on the upstairs appear to be the original to the home; they are wider planks and not in as good condition as the floors on the first level. There is a vent that goes through the ceiling of the TV/living room and through our bedroom floor that was used for a wood burning stove.

My brother and I, over the years, have shared an interest in a lot of the same hobbies and things. It was no surprise to me to find that he was interested in the paranormal, too. He has taken part in several investigations during his visits back home. The following are experiences that he shared with his wife and child while visiting my home.

The Brown Tabby

Mark's brother Luke shared:

I was visiting my brother one day with my family. We were all chatting in his bedroom. Mark and his wife, Kat, were talking about the paranormal research society that they were starting. They both have had many paranormal experiences even in their own home.

I was sitting by the doorway on the hardwood floor. I was facing the interior of the room, my back to the hallway with the door open. I had a certain feeling overcome me so I turned my head to look down the hallway. I saw a brown tabby cat. It was standing near me just outside of the doorway looking at me and then suddenly it vanished. As I told everyone in the room what I'd just seen, Kat started to flip out. I'd just described her childhood cat.

Steven and the Girl

Luke also wrote:

While visiting my home town, I decided to stop by my brother's house. I took my wife and son (three years old at the time) with me. My son has autism and doesn't react like a normal child. He just started pointing, which is unusual for an autistic child. He would point at different objects and you would tell him what it was. It is his way of asking the question, "What is this?" You can also ask him a question such as, "Where is the ball?" and he would point to the ball. If you ask him a question about an object he does not know, or if that object is not in his vicinity, then he would ignore your request.

We were all upstairs chatting. Mark was talking about his recent experiences with what Mark and Kat believe is a ghost of a young girl who seems to hang around Kat's office most of the time. My son Steven was acting a bit strange in their house, as if he were seeing something. He would look intently or even laugh while facing a direction where we all saw that nothing was there. I asked him a question, "Where is the little girl?" He responds by pointing down the stairs. A few minutes later, when Steven was running back and forth in the upstairs hallway giggling, I asked him again, "Where is the little girl?" This time he turns around and walks down the hallway and points into Kat's office.

Lump on the Bed...

It was late on a Thursday night when I settled down into bed. My wife was already fast asleep; I was still very much awake and alert when it happened. I was lying on my side facing my wife when I had the sensation of something sitting on the bed up against the back of my legs. I first dismissed it thinking, "It must be the dog..." Then I realized that the bedroom door was closed and that the dog was outside the room.

The thing at my legs was heavy and I could feel the pressure of it sitting on the bed. It was almost immediately after I made the realization that the dog was not in the room that whatever it was moved from the bed. It didn't startle me much, and it wasn't long after that that I fell asleep.

Kat's Quick Stories

A Cloaked Figure

Soon after moving into our house I had several odd experiences. I stepped outside to take the dog for a walk and I felt as if I had stepped into a whole different time period. As I walked, I noticed a man in a long cloak and an interesting top hat. My first thought was that it was just a tall Goth kid, but then I noticed some young ladies dressed in Victorian-style mourning dresses.

When I heard the clip clop of horses hooves, I startled and looked around. The dog was overly excited, but I thought she was just seeing squirrels. When she suddenly sat without me telling her to sit and was quietly wagging her tail and looking straight ahead at the same tall cloaked figure that I was seeing, I realized that something phenomenal was happening. I saw no horses, I looked around and the mysterious man and the ladies had simply disappeared.

A 40s Gal

I was getting ready to go out for a quick walk with our dog, so I was just quickly styling my hair. On this day, I was 40s inspired, so I did a twist and a roll and had the chic style of a 40s gal. So as I'm walking down the alley with the dog, I notice a young lady wearing vintage 40s clothes, so I remarked on how I liked her outfit. She said a very quiet *thank you*. The dog lunged forward, pulling my arm practically out of its socket, and as I turned back around to apologize for the dog's action, she had vanished.

I had noticed some old vintage cars in the alley and wondered who they belonged to. I looped back around with the dog and the cars were no longer there and I could not find the woman in the 40s outfit.

I was stunned at the possibilities of what had just occurred.

What Would Kolchak Do?

I was driving my car on Gay Street headed into West Chester. I was stopped at the light at the corner of Matlack when I saw a Goth kid out of the corner of my eye. It appeared he was leaning into the passenger side of my car. The next thing I know, I looked in my rearview mirror and this kid is in my car. My doors were all locked, so I freaked out and started screaming curses; and then the kid just disappeared.

Another time while driving, I was flabbergasted when in that same corner of Matlack and Gay, it felt as if someone had thwacked my head. Its funny and sad because I had just heard on the radio that Darren McGavin had passed away (My husband and I have always enjoyed the *Kolchak: The Night Staker* series) and I remember saying to myself, "So how would Kolchak respond to being thwacked in the head by an unforeseen force?" and I got thwacked again! I looked in my rearview mirror, but no one was there. I just kept driving and thought that my mind was just playing tricks on me.

Red-Plaid Visitor

In our house, I sometimes see this quick glimpse of a man wearing a red-plaid shirt in the upstairs of our house. I got very freaked out while taking a shower; I was reaching for the shampoo bottle and saw a face looking back at me. I shrieked, thinking we had an intruder in the house. Carefully stepping out and throwing my robe on immediately, I looked around, but no one else was home, and there was no sign of an intruder.

One night, as I was trying to fall asleep, I shot up startled because there was a man wearing that same red-plaid shirt staring at me. After a few minutes, I had calmed myself and I was lying back down when I saw this hand, not mine and not my husband's, coming at my face and touching my face.

Ticklish

When we first moved into the house, I was just exhausted. While sleeping, my feet would stick out from under the covers and I would feel this ice cold finger tickle them. I'd tell my husband to *knock it off* and he would get upset, saying, "No dear, that wasn't me."

Running Child

I was lying on the bed facing the door and writing in my journal when, all of a sudden, I glanced up to see a young girl wearing pigtails standing in the hallway. She was giggling and running straight towards me. I got incredible chills and tried not to panic. Once she reached the bed, she disappeared.

Laundry Help?

One day while putting clothes away after doing laundry, the closet door was wide open, blocking my whole view of the hallway. The phone rang only once; my husband had gotten it, so I continued to put clothes away in the closet. I heard these running steps coming up the stairs and stopping behind the closet door. I moved the door and no one was there. My husband had been downstairs on the phone that whole time, so I know it was not him.

Look At Me!!!

Over the course of a few nights, both my wife and I had shared the experience of something standing at the end of the bed and pounding its fists onto the bed on both sides of our legs. They felt like small fists as if from a child trying to get our attention. It was a rapid pounding sensation that shook the end of the bed. It happened for several nights and we both experienced it at different times. My wife said that at one time she felt as though there was a little girl standing at the end of the bed and desperately trying to get our attention... "Look at me! Look at me!"

The Smell of Perfume is in the Air

CCPRS had just begun to conduct experiments for our first research study, the nature and effects of table tipping, pendulum scrying, video feedback loops, and using white noise to add to the ambience of a room for conducting EVP research. These early experiments have been conducted at our home after our monthly group meetings.

It was several days to a week before our scheduled meeting/research study experiments that we started having an encounter with an old woman who was seen and heard in our bedroom. My wife had fully awakened to the sight of the woman leaning in over the bed at the end of the bed on her side. It was an elderly woman, short in stature, and dressed in clothing that was reminiscent of the mid to late 1800s. The woman was reaching out with a hand, beckoning to her, but was not heard—only seen.

Several nights later, I heard an elderly woman's voice call out my name. It was slow and deliberate. "Mark…" the voice called out, so close to me that I immediately sat up to look and see where it came from. The voice originated from my side of the bed and in or near the corner of the room closest to the bed. I turned to see if my wife was awake and had heard it, but she was already sleeping.

That following Saturday night, we had our monthly meeting with the group. The investigators present that night during our research experiment were Carol, Kim, Kat, and Myself. The focus of the research experiment that night would be with using a Pendulum in attempts to communicate with a spirit.

Kat led us through the experiment and gave us instructions on how the pendulum would work. The Pendulum works very similar to the talking board or Ouija board. A card is laid out that has the complete alphabet from left to right in a semi-circle pattern. Questions are asked and the pendulum will swing over individual letters that will spell out the response. The basic response for the pendulum is when it swings clockwise for "yes" and counterclockwise for "no." We had an ELF (extremely low frequency) zone meter set up on a tripod in the doorway between the TV room and the reading room. The purpose of the meter set in the location was so that it would track any changes in the environment, if something might pass by it.

We started asking very simple questions to see if we would get any response and it would be just a little matter of time before something would come through. A woman made her presence known to us through the pendulum. She answered some basic questions that helped us determine who she was. Her name was Mary Ross and she was born in 1862 (according to the pendulum). She claimed that she was my grandfathers' biological mother, but mathematically it was not possible, considering how old she would have been when he was born.

Despite the inaccuracy in the date, she claimed to have a message for me: "Stay in the band!" the pendulum spelled out one letter at a time. (I am a musician and I was struggling about my role in a group of which I am a part.) She also claimed that it would be at least a year or more before anything would happen with the group. I, being skeptical, was leery of what was communicating with us was actually what it claimed to be. The date of her birth was too long before date of my grandfather's birth, and that was something that raised suspicion in me right away. Before we ended our conversation with her, we asked her to give us another sign of her presence, and before any of us could react, the smell of perfume came into the room. At nearly the same time, we all remarked at the fragrance that was now in the air around us. Just as quickly as it came, it also went, and we were left puzzled by what had happened and who it was we were communicating with.

Dinah Roseberry, author of *Ghosts of Valley Forge and Phoenixville, Cape May Haunts,* and *Spooky York, Pennsylvania* and investigator for the Chester County Paranormal Research Society, had her first professional exposure with the use of a pendulum at a séance held at my home. Though she'd been systematically exposed to the tool over the years, and has since had much success with it, this was the first opportunity for an in-training experience with sensitive and author Katharine Sarro.

She says about the experience:

"The first thing I realized about using a pendulum was that not only does the instrument have to speak directly to it's user—in this case, Kat—in some ethereal connective response, but that the user's personal energy is of the utmost importance to that connection. It's interesting that spirit will specifically follow the directions set down by the person using the tool—Kat explained that clockwise rotation would reflect a *yes* answer and counterclockwise would indicate *no*. The session effectively gave insight into some personal issues that have since proved to be true.

This, too, was the time that I learned about the importance of putting protections in place prior to using such a tool. There's no telling who will be answering if you don't—especially, for us that night, since the house we were in was so haunted!

After learning the technique at this juncture, I have found that my personal protective spirits—I call them my high spirit committee—give the most reliable answers during my investigations, though, I've interacted with some spirit energy directly. The strongest responses—and the most believable—come from those who protect me.

Learning this was an important part of my training as an investigator for the team."

Katharine
during one of
the pendulum
experiments.
This picture
was taken as the
pendulum was
reacting to our
questions.

The Old Bureau

My wife and I had been living in the house in West Chester for only a few weeks when my relatives from whom we were renting the house gave us a bureau to use while we were living there. The bureau had come from an estate sale where they had purchased it at an auction. The original owner of the bureau was an older gentleman who owned and operated an antique and antique restoration business in town. My relatives had had several dealings with him with the restoration of some of their antique furniture that they had collected. The man used to be a preacher, now retired and running his own business.

A tragic fate befell him; he committed suicide as the result of being rejected by a woman. His heart was broken and he could not bear the pain. The business used to be down the alley from where our house is located. At first, we did not know the full story of where the bureau had came from, and honestly, knowing the history of it at the time was not important. We were happy to have it to use considering the lack of closet space in the house.

Our cats began to act in a strange and unusual way. When they were out in the yard they would sit in the back corner of the yard facing towards the corner. The fence is a solid privacy fence that stands about seven to eight feet tall. They would sit and stare up at something, staring about halfway up the fence. The proximity to the fence was so that it was not as if they were looking at something beyond the fence, but staring right into it or at least the upper half. It was as if they had put themselves in *time out* for bad behavior. They would sit and sit, sometimes for up to an hour, motionless and staring at the fence. I would go

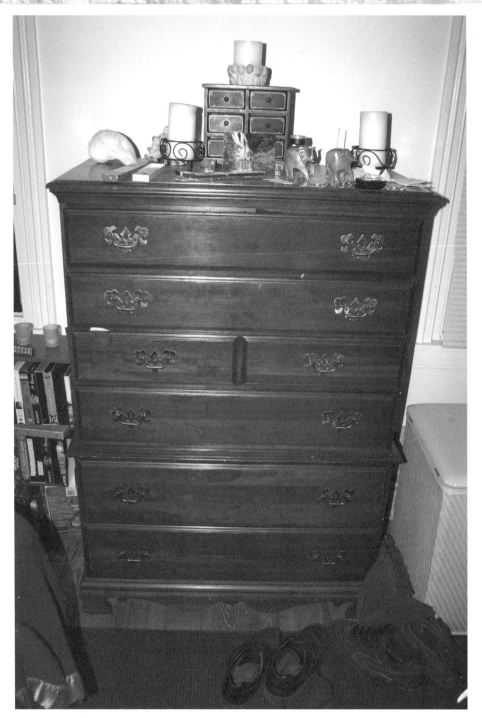

The bureau that once belonged to the shop keeper that
now sits in our bedroom.

to the back door sometimes and just stand there watching them, calling out to them to get their attention. Sometimes they would turn and look at me and other times they would ignore me altogether.

It wasn't too long before the dog started behaving in the same way. Again, I would stop and watch to see what the dog was looking at. She would sit, wagging her tail, looking up into the fence as if someone was standing there in front of her. It wasn't until my wife happened to witness the events that she swore she saw an older man standing in the corner of the yard and dressed as a priest or something of that nature. There was a time that she saw him in the house and at first she thought that someone had broken in and she ran in fright, but when she turned back he was gone.

We didn't really suspect anything with the bureau until during one of our investigations at the house. Some of our team members were holding a vigil (a period of time where investigators sit and wait, hoping for something to happen in the realm of the paranormal) and conducting an EVP session in our bedroom, when they started reading an EMF field coming off the bureau. The bureau had nothing on it or in it that would cause it to give off an EMF reading. Artificial EMF fields are caused by AC current that is being given off from lighting, wires, or appliances. The bureau had nothing of the sort that would cause it to give these unusual readings.

It wasn't too long after that, that the man seen in the yard was seen in the bedroom near the bureau. I found it odd that a bureau would give off such readings without

The corner of the yard where often a spirit has been seen.
The animals of the house will sit staring into the corner as
if they are looking at someone.

any artificial cause, and with the increased activity with a man dressed in priest-type clothing, I asked my relatives about the origin of the bureau.

The bureau was something that the older gentleman had personally owned, and when he died, it became a part of an estate sale that my relatives had purchased. Is the object haunted? Not likely, but for some reason it has attracted the man to our home. We will still see him from time to time, but he comes and goes with less frequency. The animals don't sit in the corner of the yard like they used to and his presence has been fairly quiet.

A Cry From Beyond...

The same night of the fragrance filling the room, we had other experiences as well. We started by conducting several vigils and EVP sessions before going into the research experiment using the pendulum. Carol and I were holding a vigil on the second floor in Kat's office at the back of the house. This room was of particular interest because of some of the experiences that occurred. Carol was operating her Digital still camera and an EMF meter. I had a stationary mini DV camcorder set up in the room, a thermometer for measuring the ambient temperature, and an aural enhancing listening device that was tied into a digital voice recorder.

Meanwhile, on the first floor, Kim and Kat were investigating in the living room area with their own equipment (video camera, EMF, still camera, etc). Carol and I had just begun an EVP Q&A session in the hopes to record a response from whatever it was that was in the room. I was monitoring the digital recorder via headphones through the listening device. I started asking questions aloud and asking for some sign that it was there.

"Knock on the wall; scratch on the ceiling, make some kind of noise to let us know that you are here…" I asked aloud.

Carol sat in silence across from me while taking a picture to document the event. Nothing happened. An EVP is rarely heard in real time, meaning that you usually aren't aware that you caught something on tape until you are listening in playback mode, but on some occasions, it will make a noise in response that you can hear right there as it happens. Our hope was to achieve both, that it would make some form of noise in direct response to our questions and answer us on the recording that we would hear in playback. I slowly scanned the room with the listening device.

Carol spoke up. "Did you hear that? It sounds like music!"

I turned to her with the device to see if it would be detected, I could hear it but said to her that it sounded like it was coming from outside the room, and even outside the house at that. We settled down and then I asked another question.

"If you're here, please talk to us, what is your name?"

Silence again filled the room. We typically will wait between thirty and sixty seconds before asking another question. It gives time for what might be present to respond.

"What is your name?" I asked.

In a matter of a few moments, the sounds of heavy footsteps could be heard coming up the stairs and down the hallway towards the door of the room we were in. In my headphones it was a massive sound, filling my ears.

I turned to Carol and asked her. "DO YOU HEAR THAT?" I exclaimed.

"Yes!" she replied.

It stopped and immediately I picked up the two-way radio and called down to Kat and Kim who were working downstairs.

"Kim? Did either you or Kat just come up the stairs?" I asked.

"Mark, please repeat," Kat replied over the radio.

"Did either of you just come up the stairs and down the hallway?" I asked again.

"No. Why?" Kat asked.

"We just had something stomping up the stairs and it came down the hallway and stopped outside the door!" I said.

We were amazed by the fact that something had come up the steps and down the hallway and to the door, just stopping outside of it. I was excited, because I knew that I caught it on audio and hoped that it came out on video as well.

In the days that followed that evening's investigation, I was reviewing the audio and video from that night. The video did not reveal the sound of the footsteps as clearly as I had hoped, but when I reviewed the audio recording made with the aural enhancer, I was shocked to find a female moan made just shortly before the footsteps stopped. It was clear and came from within the room! I knew with certainty that it was not Carol or anyone else within the house and it certainly was not me. This EVP is available and can be heard online at: www.chestercountyprs.com/evp.htm.

The Portal Experiments

It was in the very beginning of CCPRS' existence that I started to conduct research experiments with white noise, video feedback loops, strobe lights, pendulums and tone generators. I had come across a Web site mentioned in several online forums that purportedly was a portal run by psychics and mediums in a way to communicate with the other side. I wish not to name the site because, despite my mixed feelings on what the Web site claims, it does appear to have some affect that if one is not careful, may lead to more dangerous experiences.

I was intrigued and immediately began to visit the Web site and record the audio signal that I was streaming from the site. My curiosity for these things has gotten me into trouble before, but it has always been a part of my nature to jump into something and stir the pot before realizing what was in the pot that I'd just jumped in to. I would listen intently with a pair of headphones and try to determine if there was any specific pattern to the sound. It was white noise, but it seemed to have a distinct pattern.

My first few initial experiments yielded nothing more then a slight headache from the continuous monitoring of the noise generated on the Web site. It wasn't until my third or fourth experiment that I noticed that there was something else within the pattern that was completely random. It was if something was trying to come through the noise, but it was indecipherable and not any kind of voice, but a break in the pattern. I can't really describe it, other then a variation in the noise that was a constant.

In the beginning of these experiments, I was completely alone in my research. Katharine and I would use the white noise in conjunction with some EVP work that we were do-

Aural Enhancer that was used to capture the EVP in the office.

ing at the house. We had been concentrating on the second floor of the home, in the hallway just outside the master bedroom. I would have the Web site open while we had a microphone connected to the same recording software that was recording the white noise from the Web.

We would ask our questions during the EVP sessions and the response would come from a break in the pattern on the white noise. It was inconsistent at best and we never captured any disembodied voices or other patterns through the microphone we used to record the EVP sessions.

The experiments began to increase in size and number. I began to include other members of the group as a part of the experiment and it would grow to include other research techniques that I considered "experimental" and not part of the norm for research/investigation protocol with CCPRS.

This is where the experiments with a video feedback loop would come into play coupled with the white noise generated from the Web site that I was researching. I also began to experiment with a tone generator that I would use to play specific frequencies through an amplifier in a room to affect the environment making it conducive to EVP experiments. I also had read about the use of a strobe light with a filter attached while taking pictures in the environment where the strobe light was focused. I had doubts about some of these techniques, but was still curious to see if we would have any positive results. We would conduct these experiments at the end of our monthly meetings taking place in the house.

The video feedback loop consisted of a video camera connected directly to a television, set up on a tripod and pointed back at the television while the camera was on. The effect would create a looping pattern that would randomize and change. I would also manipulate the patterns in the loop by changing the angle of the camera and zoom settings on the lens. I had read several books and articles that had mentioned using this technique with the desired result of capturing ghostly images on the television of something or someone from the other side.

I wanted to find out for myself if there was any merit with these kinds of techniques. It was now, at this point, that I began to run the white noise from the Web site through the stereo in the room where we had the video feedback loop setup. I flooded the room with the white noise from the site to see what effect it would have on the experiment as a whole.

I felt that I was starting to get some results with the research I was conducting and it seemed to have a direct effect on the activity in the house. I had made the connection that the more frequently I visited the Web site and listened; the more frequently things began to happen—which, unfortunately, can turn into a dangerous pursuit. I was basically opening up a door and inviting *in* whatever wanted to come through.

Over the years of research and study in this field, on my own and with a group, I have found myself in these kinds of situations. I did not fear it and felt confident about how to handle things when they started to get to a point where it was *too much*. And not too long after these experiments began, it started to become too much.

My wife and I knew early on that the house we were living in was quite active and had a few "regulars," but with the increased activity, research and active investigations at the home by members of my group and myself, we started noticing that there was a lot more then just what had become the norm for the activity in the house. It soon would escalate to the point where all investigations, research, or any other active study of the home would come to a screeching halt—but I digress. I will come back to those events soon enough.

The strobe lights, for the most part, did little more then give myself and the other investigators a headache from being exposed to it for too long.

I had also been using the tone generator along with the strobe light. The tone generator was set to send out a steady tone at 200 hertz. I had set the tone generator to a lower frequency with the hope that it would have an effect on any EVP sessions that we conducted during these experiments. We kept the strobe light/tone generator experiments limited to the upstairs hallway in the house so not to disturb the experiments that we were conducting down stairs with the white noise and video feedback. There are a few pictures of interest that were a direct result of the strobe light experiment.

I began to experience some strange physical side effects from the long-term exposure to the white noise experiments. I found myself feeling very tired and having the sensation of being in a fog or some sort of haze. My thoughts were not clear and I had a very unsettling feeling about me whenever I was in the house. My wife, too, had begun to become more distressed by the dramatic increase in activity. I knew that I had gone too far with the white noise experiments when, on one particular weekend when my younger brother had been visiting, we decided to take it one step further than I had gone before with the previous experiments.

My brother, as I mentioned earlier, has shared the interest that I have with science, the weather, and the paranormal. On this particular weekend when we conducted the experiment, I had flash backs to our child hood when we would run around the house in the dark with our flashlights, hunting ghosts and setting traps to see what we would attract. Of course, it was all in fun because that house was not haunted. Well, on this particular night, we had decided to use multiple computers to stream the audio from this particular Web site. I believe that we had four computers in all that were on and connected to the site, with my main laptop connected to the stereo that would push the signal throughout the room.

I had also set up the video feedback loop with the camera and recorded what was being seen through the camera. My brother took many photos and we held vigil, waiting to see what, if anything, would happen.

One of the worst things that I think anyone could do in this situation would be to fall asleep. Unfortunately, this is something that I did. I was falling in between sleep and consciousness, continuously teetering on the edge of a dream-like state. There were a few moments where I did completely fall asleep and would find myself jolted awake by something in the room. My brother sat on the couch opposite the TV and sat in silence. I believe he too at times started to drift off asleep.

The entire experiment lasted several hours that night and finally it came to be going on four in the morning when I finally roused enough consciousness to realize that we had to end the experiment and call it a night.

The next day was a day that I struggled with my ability to have clear thoughts; I felt weighed down and at times confused. I was in a state that I could not shake; it made me feel like I did after having a sleep seizure. (A sleep seizure or focal seizure is where the body is asleep but the mind is awake and lucid, almost in a dreaming state. I used to have these types of seizures frequently in my late teens and early twenties. They were brought on by stress and a severe lack of sleep. At the time of this incident with the portal experiment, I had not had a sleep seizure in well over a year or more.) My brother reported no strangeness or issues with himself. I kept my thoughts and feelings to myself most of that day, mainly because I was struggling to understand why I was feeling the way that I did. It was the start of something much more that would soon cause alarm to me, my wife, and other members of the group.

…To be continued.

Living room. *Photo by Luke Sarro*

Darlington Street on the block
where the house is located.

The living room and street side room of the house. Katharine was motioning to something in the corner at the time of the picture. The Orb is hovering just above her hand. *Photo by Luke Sarro.*

Living room with orb. *Photo by Luke Sarro.*

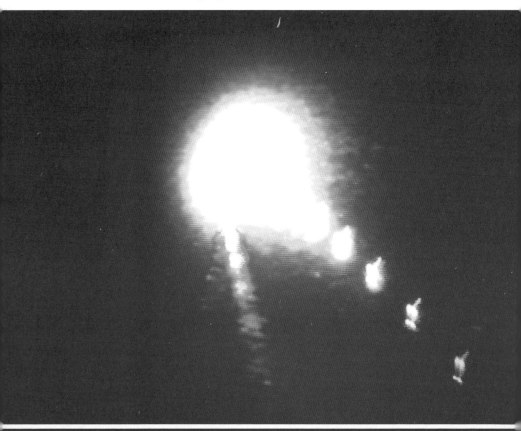

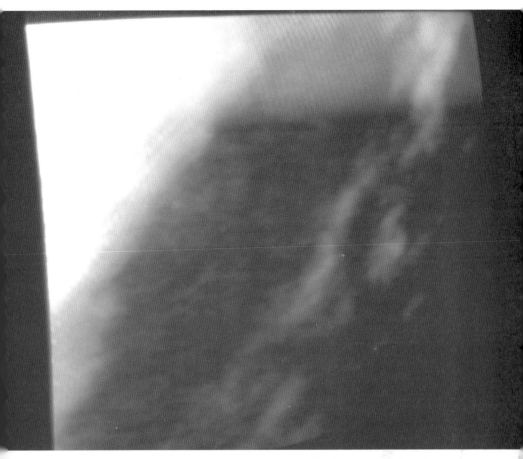

Left, Top: Another photo of the video feedback experiment. This is an example of a swell of light caused by the video camera looping back into itself.

Left. Bottom: This photo was taken during the video feedback experiments. Notice the trail of light coming off of it and going down to the left.

Luke took this photo during the July experiments. The image of a face can be seen to the left of the image as a profile. Is this an example of matrixing or is it a genuine image coming through as a result of the experiment?

Section 6

The Inhuman/Demonic Haunting

An Inhuman or Demonic Haunting involves a spirit that has never walked the earth as a living being, but is something that has always been in another realm and place of existence. There are many sub categories of the inhuman entity, but our focus is on the negative, or one that is of a demonic nature. The Inhuman/ Demonic Haunting is considered, among those in the paranormal community, as on the fringe. There is lots of controversy surrounding reported cases.

In my opinion, this is the only type of haunting that has the potential for negative long-term effects for anyone who might come in contact with the activity, whether being a member of a family who is experiencing it or an investigator/researcher who may be helping out with the case.

There are psychic/mediums and investigators who will emphatically deny that this type of haunting actually exists, but I believe that it really takes a personal firsthand experience to really understand the full nature of this kind of activity. The demonic/inhuman is like an infection that finds its way into someone's life and slowly takes over, beginning to reek havoc over those who are directly involved.

I have had several experiences in various ways with this kind of haunting over the years of my informal and formal investigating. To this day, these are the only kinds of experiences that I have had that have truly frightened me and made me realize just how dangerous getting involved with these kinds of cases can be.

My group doesn't actively seek out these types of cases, but when we come across them, we proceed with extreme caution, and if need be, will refer them out to someone who specializes.

Lurking in the Darkness

This story of an experience came to me via an email that I received through the CCPRS Web site. The gentleman contacted me asking if I needed more stories and told me that he would like to share one with me. I had exchanged my contact information with him and we spoke very briefly via phone to set up a time to meet so that I could hear his story. I have decided to present this story as closely to the way that he told it, from his perspective. I will touch on elements of his story at the end and give some of my personal thoughts as to the events that took place leading up to the experiences he had, and our eventual meeting for his retelling of the story.

We decided to meet at the diner on West Chester pike just outside of town. I arrived and met him outside of the restaurant. He was about 5'9" and stocky, his hair dark with patches of gray. He was a bit disheveled and wore a pair of jeans, dark t-shirt with a light jacket. He was smoking a cigarette and pacing a bit when I first approached him.

"Jack?" I questioned as I stepped up to him.

"Yeah…" he replied.

"Hey. I'm Mark, from CCPRS," I said as I stepped forward and reached out my hand to shake his. We shook hands and he didn't say much. I followed him into the restaurant and we grabbed a booth in one of the windows at the front of the diner. I pulled out my notebook from my bag and waited for him to speak.

"It was a long time ago…" he pauses, takes a drag from his cigarette and say while exhaling. "I still have trouble with it to this day… It never really leaves."

"I am not sure I understand what you are saying," I replied.

"What do you mean? I thought that you were an expert in this field?" he retorted.

"There are no experts…" I said dryly.

"Oh… Well, I mean the demon…or devil, or whatever the hell you want to call it!" he barked back.

He was starting to become agitated. I didn't want him to get so worked up about it—I know that telling a tale of this sort can bring up a lot of emotions. "I don't mean to upset you; I just want to understand what happened," I said.

"Alright, I'll tell you, but I am still uncertain of what really happened."

It was the summer of 02' and my wife and I had just moved into a house in the Riggtown section of West Chester. It was a hard year, my wife had just lost her father and I was struggling with depression. I still didn't know what to feel or how to react. We had been having problems and I wasn't sure if things were going to work out for us or not. We decided to move and try and get a fresh start in a new town, and West Chester turned out to be that place.

I had found a job right away and my wife was taking some time to get adjusted before going back to work. The house was nice and everything seemed okay at first, but very quickly, things started to show that it was not quite as it seemed. In a short amount of time, I started working double shifts. I had too, we just weren't making enough money to pay for everything and my wife was just not ready to go back to work. I would be gone for many hours a day and sometimes six and seven days a week. My wife stayed in the house most of the time.

We had just moved from Ohio and all of our friends and family were there. I started to notice after a few weeks that my wife was slipping into a depression. She didn't leave the house and would sleep most of the time. Looking back, I can't imagine how alone and isolated she felt, considering that all of her friends and family were hundreds of miles away, and with me working all the time, she had no one to talk to or spend time with. She would occasionally go to the store, but that was about it. It was slow and steady, but I could tell she was getting worse.

I would get home from work sometimes about eleven or so and go right to bed, considering I would have to be at work early the next morning. I would come home and she would be sitting alone in the dark in the living room with the TV on, and sometimes she would be laying on the couch in a way where I wasn't sure if she was awake or not. I would come over to her and greet her, and most times she wouldn't respond. I would try to get her to come up to bed with me and she would practically ignore me. I'd go to bed and lay there thinking about everything that has happened and was going on. I didn't know what to do or how to help her. I saw it happening, it got worse and worse and still I did nothing.

It had been several months now and I was still working long shifts and getting home late. My wife had been the same. On my days off, I would try and get her to go with me to the store, or go and spend the day somewhere, or even just go for a walk—and she would refuse. I tried once, almost to the point of physically getting her up off of the couch, and she hit and scratched me as though I was trying to hurt her. I got so mad that I stormed out of the house and didn't come home until many hours and a few beers later.

That is when I realized that something else was going on. My wife had turned into someone who I didn't know anymore, I would see this person and occasionally she would sleep next to me in bed, but I didn't know her. She didn't talk to me, and most nights, she would be up all night or sleep on the couch. There were a few times that I would get up in the morning and she would still be up and lying on the couch in front of the TV.

Well, that night...the night that I came home after storming out, it was different. I came in the house, went straight up the stairs, and went to bed. I didn't want to talk to her and I didn't want to deal with it. I was feeling the beers and exhausted from the many long days that I just worked. I was lying in bed and had just started to drift off to sleep when I heard it... There were voices talking in a low murmur and they sounded like they were just outside of the room.

I jumped out of the bed and threw open the door and looked up and down the hallway. I went down the hallway and down the stairs and found my wife asleep on the couch and the TV was off. I turned and went back to bed dismissing it as a lucid dream or something like that.

It wasn't more then a few moments before I heard them again. This time, I laid there listening and trying to understand what was being said. I suddenly became overwhelmed with a feeling of dread and was paralyzed in my bed. I couldn't move and it took every effort that I had to keep myself breathing. It felt as though something was sitting on my chest, and I suddenly felt as though a surge of electricity was coursing through my body. I could hear a buzzing or some kind of hum in my ears and the murmurs that I was hearing in the hallway had started to work into a frenzy of whispers and voices.

Out of the corner of my eye, a shadow was forming in the corner of the room; I managed to turn myself to face it straight on and watched it as it took shape into some unknown form. It was in that moment that everything stopped and I was able to sit up, and the whispers, the shadow, and that feeling of dread and cold had passed. I pulled myself out of bed and ran into the bathroom and began to throw up. I was consumed by nausea and a sick feeling in my stomach.

I made my way back to bed and fell to my face and passed out where I lie.

The next morning I awoke with a horrible headache, and the nausea and stomach cramps were still there, but not as intense as they were the night before. Now, I know what you're thinkin'. I was drunk and hung over… Well, I tell ya', I wasn't; I know how I felt and I didn't drink that much to be that tore up and affected the next day. I showered, dressed, and made my way downstairs.

My wife was awake and sitting on the couch. She looked as though she hadn't showered or changed clothes for days. She was still in the same pair of sweats and t-shirt that I had seen her in for the past week or so. I went past her and into the kitchen to start some coffee and grab a bowl of cereal or something. She then spoke in a low muttered voice; I couldn't understand what she was saying. I walked out of the kitchen and stood near her…

"What did you say? I didn't hear ya?" I asked.

"I have been told that you met my friends last night." She spoke without any emotion.

"What the HELL are you talking about???" I stammered.

"My friends…" She spoke again in a low soft voice.

"HUH? Your FRIENDS! What the F do you mean? …my friends?" I screamed.

She turned to look at me, smiled a dry smirk, and shook her head. In that brief moment our eyes met and her eyes were black as coals! I didn't recognize who she was; this was not my wife! I fell back in disbelief and uncertainty. The nausea hit me with full force again and I found myself running for the bathroom again and getting sick. I spent a good half hour in the bathroom before I could pull myself together. The pounding in my head intensified again and I was consumed with fear and feelings of dread.

My wife was no longer on the couch and the TV was off. I checked the kitchen and then went upstairs to see where she was. I found her in the bedroom sitting on the end of the bed and staring blankly into nothing. I called out to her and she did not respond. I stood in the doorway and waited. I called out to her again and still nothing.

She turned again to face me, and instantly, I felt two heavy hands push me—into my chest—and I was thrown back and into wall on the other side of the doorway in the hall. The bedroom door slammed shut as I fell to the floor.

I laid there stunned, but knew that something had to be done and that I had to get out of there. I picked myself up and ran down the stairs, grabbed my keys, and stormed out of the house.

I wandered around town in a daze; I couldn't believe what was happening and I surely didn't understand. It was like a nightmare and I couldn't wake up. "My friends?" I thought to myself. What has she gotten herself into? What is going on?

I ended up in the downtown and sat on a park bench near the corner of Church and Gay Street. It was a bright and sunny day and the street was full of activity, with people going by and traffic, but it was all a blur. I don't really know how long I sat there or what I must have looked like. I was dazed and feeling uncertain about everything.

What am I supposed to do? I don't have any friends here, my family is far away. I only have my wife. Several more hours had passed and by now the sun was starting to set. I was still walking around town, now feeling a little less dazed, but still unsure. I made my way into a neighborhood bar and took refuge. I began to drink, the beers kept coming. I think there was a game on one of TVs in the bar that I would stare at from time to time. I kept to myself at the end of the bar. It was a typical Saturday night there. The bar slowly started to fill up as the night progressed. It was getting too crowded for my own good and I found myself back on the street again. I had been drinking for several hours or more and was out of cash and felt that it was time to go home and face whatever it was that was there.

It took a while before I could get up the courage to put the key in the door and open it and go in. I pushed the door open slowly and saw that she was not on the couch in her usual position. The house was dark and there was a light fragrance of something that I could not make out hanging in the air. It was a pleasant smell, and I couldn't tell what or where it was coming from.

I put my keys on the table by the door, stepped in, and closed the door softly behind me. I headed up the stairs and made my way to the bedroom, but my attention was drawn to the other bedroom door just off to my right. The door was closed, but not all the way. A low flickering light came through the cracks in the door and out from under it. I stepped up to it slowly and tried to see what was going on in the room without disturbing the door. I couldn't really see, but I saw my wife sitting on the floor in front of the dresser that we had on the one wall by the door. I could see several candles lit and placed about the room. She was focused on the floor in front of her and was doing something with her hands; I could not tell. I watched as she was muttering and mumbling to herself, and swaying slowly back and forth. She looked as though she was in a trance or something. It was a strange sight and I didn't really understand it.

I tried to shift my weight from one foot to the other and lean in a way that I could see better what she was doing. I slipped and fell into the door, pushing it open towards the dresser and causing a lamp to crash to the floor inside the room. In that instant, I felt myself being bombarded with slaps and punches and scratches. She was on me in a fury, screaming and clawing at me, and pushing me at the same time.

I scrambled to my feet and fled from the room. She was in pursuit behind me, but stopped as soon as I crossed the threshold of the door. I was moving so fast that I crashed into the wall in the hallway opposite of the door. I caught myself and then quickly turned back to see why she had stopped. She was standing there, motionless, staring at me.

Her eyes were black and seemed to have no pupils. She stepped back and the door slammed shut by itself.

I then heard it lock and that was it.

I was too tired to leave the house and go somewhere else; instead I made my way to the bedroom and closed and locked the door behind me. I grabbed the chair from her make-up table and propped it up against the door and under the door knob so that it would reinforce the locked door. I wasn't taking any chances. I crawled into bed and found myself asleep no sooner than I had laid my head down.

I awoke in a panic to the sounds of scratching and knocking on the bedroom door. I sat straight up and saw the same flickering light that was inside the other bedroom just outside of the bedroom door. It sounded as though many fists were pounding on the door and the scratching sounds seemed to be inside the room and coming from every direction. The smell of something rotten filled my nostrils and began to turn my stomach. The whispering began and the low guttural voices were in the hallway again.

I backed myself up against the wall on the bed and sat there. The sounds and smell was all about me and had sent a chill through me. I found myself shivering, as though I had been out in the freezing cold. The temperature in the room dropped so suddenly that I could see my breath. The voices got louder and the pounding became more intense.

A voice was cutting through over all of the others and sounded as though it was in my head. "Let us in…Let us in…" it said over and over again. I tried to ignore it and pretend that I was not hearing it or experiencing what I was, but there was no stopping it.

I turned and looked at the clock; it was a half past three in the morning. The assault continued through the night, and slowly the intensity decreased as daybreak was approaching. Once the sun had finally started to come up, it had all but stopped. I was weak and drained from keeping guard during the night. I kept my eyes fixed on the door and would not let myself drift off to sleep, but now there was no fighting it. I was asleep in no time.

I woke up at about 11:30 am and pulled myself out of bed. To my surprise the bedroom door was wide open and the chair that I had used to reinforce it had been smashed to bits. Pieces of the chair were scattered about the room. I went into the bathroom to splash some water on my face. I looked into the mirror and found three scratch marks had been made across my face, from above my right eye down across my face and nose and to the side of my face. Something had gotten into the room and marked me.

I quickly washed my face, toweled off, and left the room. I crept slowly down the hallway and came across the bedroom door where the events had taken place the night before. The door was closed, but slightly cracked as it was before. I stood before it and contemplated whether or not I wanted to open the door and see what was in the room. I didn't really give myself a chance to reconsider and pushed the door open slowly.

There was no sign of her anywhere in the room. I stepped in, looked around again, and stepped closer to the dresser she had been sitting in front of. I could see the remnants of two candles that had burned all the way down and were sitting on the floor. The wax had melted into two pools and was hardened on the hard wood floor. I knelt down to take a closer look at them.

Out of the corner of my eye, I caught a glimpse of something sitting underneath the dresser. It was flat and had something sitting on top of it that I could not make out. I reached for it and was able to pull it out from under the dresser. It was a board that was about the size of a door mat. There was the alphabet spelled out, letter for letter, across the board, the numbers 0-9 and a *yes, no* or *maybe* on the board as well. It appeared to be homemade and was on a piece of wood that may have been a part of some furniture or something like that.

The thing sitting on top of the board was some kind of stained-glass piece that reminded me of something that someone would hang in the window of a house. It wasn't very big, about four inches or so. In the design of the piece was a five pointed star that sat in a circle. The piece itself was propped up on three little legs that allowed it to sit just above the board.

I didn't really know what this was; I had never seen it before. I decided to push it back under the dresser and leave it be. I didn't want to disturb it too much out of fear of what might happen. This must have been what my wife was working with on the floor last night as I saw her. I rose and turned, leaving the room and pulling the door back to how I found it. I continued down the hall and down the stairs. I found my wife fast asleep on the couch, as it had been for many weeks now. I went to the door, grabbed my keys, and left the house.

I had a clearer head then the day before, and now, with the night behind me, I realized that I had to do something. My wife and I weren't religious people and I especially would not consider myself to be spiritual in anyway. For some reason, it just wasn't a part of who I was, but I knew that there was something terrible going on in the house and I had the scratches on my face to prove it. I had to find help, and the only thing that came to mind was going to a church and hoping to talk to someone who might know or understand what it was that I was going through and what my wife may be involved with.

I walked towards the center of town again and found myself at a church in the heart of town. I stepped in and tried to find someone who could help me—an older fellow dressed like a priest or pastor, I am not really sure. To be honest, I can't even tell you the name of the church I was in. He welcomed me into his office and I sat down across from him at his desk. I started to tell him right away about everything that has been happening over the past few days and how my wife had slowly slipped into a depression over the past few months.

He was very empathetic and listened to everything that I had to say, but he really didn't offer much help, other then to get my wife to a counselor or psychiatrist, and that we both could use some spiritual counseling. As nice and welcoming as he was, he really didn't want to get involved anymore then he had to. I felt that a church was my only option, that someone there would know what to do or what exactly it was that was going on, but that would not be case—or at least not at the church that I was in. I thanked the priest and left as quickly as I could. It was obvious that there wouldn't be any help there.

I continued to walk around town in the hopes that something would come to me and give me a chance to figure it out, or at least find some help. I started to feel helpless. I had visited several more churches over the course of the day, and either no one wanted to hear my story or no one was even available to talk to. I had no one to turn to.

It then hit me; call my sister! She has always been into some weird spiritual stuff; maybe she would know what is going on and what I could do to stop it. I found the nearest payphone and tried to call her collect. I lucked out and she was home and able to take my call. I started spilling my guts to her before she even had a chance to ask me how I was doing.

She told me that my wife had been messing with a Ouija or talking board in an attempt to communicate with spirits or ghosts or whatever. I couldn't believe it! How did my wife get caught up in that? She and I are very similar in our beliefs and that is something that is definitely not a part of her equation.

My sister also began to tell me that the experiences I was having were that of something inhuman and could possibly be demonic. She suggested that I find some sage, get a bible, and try and bless the house.

I told her that I had no idea where to get sage and what I would even do with it. She assured me that it would be okay and said that she was going to head out my way as soon as possible and that she would help me with dealing with what was going on in the house. She said that she was going to drive and that she would arrive sometime around 10 pm tonight. I thanked her profusely and she assured me that things were going to be alright. I told her that I would not go back into the house until she arrived and that we could enter the house together. I also told her that I would find a hotel room nearby and that she should page me when she got in town so that I could call her to let her know where I was.

I decided to go back to my car and find a hotel room nearby. I really needed some rest and a hot shower would be good, too. I found a hotel within a mile of town on south High Street and Route 202. I checked into the room, took a shower, and then lay down on the bed and tried to sleep for a few hours. It was about 6 pm and I had a few hours before my sister would arrive and felt that some much needed sleep was in order.

I awoke to the sound of my pager going off. I looked up and reached over to grab it off the nightstand next to the bed. The clock said 10:13 pm. I looked at the pager and the number was local, it was my sister. I got up and grabbed the phone and called the number on the pager. My sister answered the phone and we spoke briefly. I told her where I was and what room I was in, and she said that she was on her way.

It was about fifteen minutes later when the knock came on my door. I opened it and she came into the room. We hugged and greeted each other; I hadn't seen her since I moved out here and she couldn't have come at a better time, or worse—depending on how you look at it.

She explained to me what we were going to do and that we were going to confront something that was potentially dangerous, not only to my wife, but to us as well. I was nervous and I still didn't fully understand what was going on, despite the fact that I had witnessed it firsthand.

We were going to bless the house and attempt to cleanse it, in the hopes that the "friends" of my wife would leave. She also said that if need be, she would do a blessing over my wife and try and get her to resist the hold that whatever was in the house had on her.

It was about 11 pm before we finally arrived back at the house. I stood there, struck with fear and dread. I really didn't want to be there, and I surely didn't want to confront whatever it was in the house.

My sister waited for me to put the key in the door and turn the knob, but I didn't. I stood there hoping that there would be another way to deal with this problem. My sister had to give me a little push so that I would actually turn the key and open the door. I pushed the door open very slowly, the house was in darkness, save for a few candles that were lit about the living room. The house had an unfamiliar feeling; for a moment I couldn't believe that I had actually lived there.

We stepped through the door very slowly. I looked about with hesitation, expecting my wife to come out of nowhere and attack me again like she had before. There was no sign of her, or at least she wasn't on the first floor. My sister slowly closed the door behind her and we moved further into the room where my wife had made herself a fixture over the past several months.

The air was heavy and had a scent of something burning, but it was not strong enough to really tell what it was. My sister motioned to the stairs and I led the way. We made our way slowly up the stairs. We reached the top of the stairs and stopped at the landing on the end of the hallway. The second floor was dark, but there was a light flickering from under the door at the end of the hall.

I still wasn't absolutely sure what we were doing, but my sister assured me that we had to confront my wife and then bless the house. First, we had to find my wife. It started to seem quite clear that she was in the room at the end of the hall. I really didn't want to go in there. My wife had turned into someone who I didn't know and I could not predict how she would react.

We got closer and closer to the door at the end of the hall. I placed my hand on the door knob and waited, looked at my sister and watched for her signal. She nodded; I closed my eyes and took a deep breath, then without hesitation, threw the door open.

There she was, sitting in the middle of the room on the floor. She was surrounded by candles and she had the homemade talking board placed in front of her. She appeared to be in a trance, not startled by our entrance into the room—as a matter of fact, she didn't respond at all. The light flickered and pulsed about the room, causing shadows to twist and move, casting them in all directions. I stood there in silence waiting for what would happen next.

My sister stepped into the room and began to recite a prayer aloud while she lit the bundle of sage and began to wave it in the air about the room. In that moment, my wife turned her head towards us and opened her eyes. There was no sign of life in her, the pupils in her eyes were gone and they were black as coal. She still didn't move, but fixed her gaze upon us and observed what we were doing. I backed up and stood just behind my sister and off to the right. I did not like the way that my wife was staring at us and I became consumed with an overwhelming sense of dread.

My sister continued the prayer and made her way to a corner in the room where she began at the floor and worked her way to the ceiling with the lit bundle of sage. My wife then rose to her feet and I moved back into the wall behind me. She started laughing, but it sounded like there were many people in the room laughing with her.

The room suddenly went cold and the smell of decay filled it. My sister then reached into her pocket and pulled out a set of rosary beads and took the crucifix at the end of the beads into her hand and held it outright in front of her, pointing it in the direction of my wife. My sister looked at me and said for me to join her in reciting the *Lord's Prayer*.

We started and my wife's eyes came back to her normal color and she fell to the floor and began sobbing. My sister instructed me to kneel down and pick up my wife and carry her out of the room. I took her into our bedroom and laid her down on the bed. I rushed back to my sister's side and waited for her instructions. She said that we must go room to room and sage and bless each room; reciting the *Lord's Prayer* and making the presence of god known to the house. She said that we would have to hold vigil over my wife and recite prayers over her in an attempt to rid her of whatever it was that was taking hold of her.

She told me to gather up all of the candles and the talking board and put them in a garbage bag, and then pour salt into the bag on top of them, seal the bag and then remove it from the house. I did as she had said, gathering up all the candles that were about the house and the talking board and put them in a bag with salt poured on top of them. I took the bag and put it in the trashcan in the backyard. My sister then said to turn on all the lights in the house and then join her in the bedroom.

My wife was still lying on the bed; it seemed as though she had fallen asleep. It was now approaching three o'clock in the morning and we still had to hold vigil over my wife and make a blessing and offer prayers. The exhaustion of everything that had been happening over the last few days had started to overcome me. I suddenly felt as though I could not stand upright or keep my eyes open. I felt my legs giving out on me, and before I knew it, I fell, lying unconscious on the floor.

My sister said that as soon as I hit the floor the room took on a menacing feel, one that immediately filled her with dread. The furniture in the room began to shake, and books, pictures, and other loose items that were sitting on the desk, bureau, and night stand fell off and onto the floor. She fell to the floor to try and revive me, but something pushed her back as she did so, and it sent her flying backwards into the dresser, and she too lost consciousness.

I remember slowly coming too, but it was more like waking up from a deep sleep. I saw my sister lying on the floor, not moving and her eyes were closed. I sat up quickly and looked about the room and saw that my wife was no longer on the bed. I moved quickly over to my sister to try and wake her and help her. She too slowly woke up and sat up rubbing her head. She had hit it when she was pushed back into the dresser. She looked at me with groggy eyes and turned slowly to see if my wife was still lying on the bed.

"She's gone," I said in a quiet toneless voice.

"Have you looked for her?" she asked timidly.

"No, I just woke up and saw you and that was all..." I replied.

"What time is it?" she asked.

"Uhh, I don't know, lemme look..." I turned to look at the alarm clock... "It's 4:19," I said as I turned back towards my sister.

"We lost an hour or so?" she asked.

"I think so," I said.

"We have got to find her!" she stammered. "Where is she?" she asked again.

"Let's find her..."

I got up and then helped my sister to her feet. My sister noticed that her rosary beads were lying on the bed. She went to them and grabbed them up into her hands. The reaction was as though she had found the most precious thing in the world. She clutched them tightly in her hands. It was at that moment that she started shaking a bit. The night was starting to wear on her, and it was starting to wear on me, too, for that matter.

We began for the door, cautiously exiting the room back into the hallway. We were uncertain of what still waited for us, but my sister was resolved in doing what she had come here to do. I was starting to doubt that we would ever be able to help my wife. She had acted and done things that I could have never imagined her doing, and unfortunately, I doubt that I would ever be able to forget them.

The house was quiet, an unsettling calm, because I knew that whatever it was that has taken over my wife and home was still lurking about, waiting to make its next strike.

We moved slowly down the hall, peering into each room as we passed, and made our way for the stairs. As we got closer to the stairs, I noticed that the air became thick and dense, making it hard to breathe. There was an odor that began to come to me, a mixture of sulfur and something else that I could not make out. My sister grabbed my arm...

"Wait!" she commanded as we stopped at the top of the stairs. "Something just moved at the bottom of the stairs!" she said as she pointed down the stairs.

I looked and struggled to see as it was too dark, but before I turned back to my sister, I saw something move, but could not tell what it was. "What was that?" I asked.

"I don't know, but it's definitely not your wife," she replied. We started down the stairs, pausing after each step; each time we stopped to listen and look, but still everything was quiet. We managed to get to the bottom of the stairs without incident.

At first glance, my wife was nowhere in sight. We moved into the living room from the stairs and there she was lying on the floor, face down, in front of the couch. I raced over to her and kneeled down next to her. I rolled her over onto her back and checked to see if she was still breathing. Her breathe was shallow and I picked her up into my arms. I called out to her, over and over again, but she did not respond.

My sister was standing over us now as she glanced around the room as if she was looking for someone else. Her eyes stopped and focused on a corner of the room. I could see terror filling her eyes as they grew wider and wider. I looked up and saw that there was a massive black shapeless form in the corner where she was staring. It was like a cloud, but much denser and it was growing.

I didn't know how to react; I was in shock, confused, and wiped out by sheer exhaustion. It didn't seem to faze me. I yelled at it… "LEAVE!!! YOU ARE NOT

WELCOME HERE!!! GET OUT!" I reached for the closest thing to me and threw it at the corner. I became enraged and stood facing it. My sister stood clutching her rosary beads and began saying the *Lord's Prayer* aloud. I took a step closer to it and again began to yell. "GET OUT OF MY HOUSE!!!"

The form started to move towards me and still I did not back down. I reached down and saw the container of kosher salt sitting on the coffee table; I grabbed it and ripped the lid off of the container and began throwing the salt at the form that was coming closer. My sister was getting louder and louder as she recited the prayer over and over again. The form stopped and began to retreat back into the corner.

I stepped forward again, throwing salt at it and anything else that was in reach. I screamed again… "GET OUT OF MY HOUSE!!!"

It moved further back into the wall, and the wall began to shake as the pictures hanging on it began to crash to the floor. I threw the last of the salt and the container at the corner. It ricochets off of the corner and fell to the floor.

The form had left, disappeared. And then everything became quiet again.

I was breathing heavy now and I stopped, turned, and looked at my sister who was standing just behind me and to my left. She looked at me and then back to the corner. I turned and looked again, but it was gone. I went back to my wife, I grabbed her up again, and she slowly began to open her eyes. My sister came and kneeled down on the other side. My wife started to wake up, and as she realized that it was my sister and I, she began to cry hysterically and covered her face with her hands as she pulled away from me and curled up lying on the floor. It was over, the feeling in the house was suddenly different, and the feeling of oppression and the air itself was different.

My sister collapsed back to the couch and I sat next to her and watched as my wife continued crying and motioned for us to stay away. Later that morning, my sister and I helped my wife up and got her out of the house and into my car. We drove to the hospital and brought her into the emergency room. We didn't know what else to do. She had stopped crying, but remained still, wide eyed and staring, but no longer responding to anything or anyone.

It was later that morning that my wife was committed to a mental hospital for evaluation. My wife never really fully recovered and remained in the hospital for several months. Our marriage ended as a result of it; she is now living with her brother in Texas and I no longer live in the area either. I sold the house not long after she left for Texas and I then left myself.

I now live in Jersey, about two hours from here.

(I interrupted him at this point.) "What brought you back to the area?" I asked.

"I still had a few things in storage that I had forgotten about until I got a notice from the place saying that they were going to throw my stuff out. I saw your flyer in the supermarket and decided to contact you," he replied.

"Have you had any more experiences with anything since the house?" I asked.

"No, it's been quiet." He spoke quietly.

"What about your wife?" I asked.

"I don't know; we haven't talked for months. The last I heard she was back in a hospital out in Texas; she had another breakdown," he replied.

"I am sorry to hear it," I said.

"Don't worry about it..." he said. As he began to reach for his cigarettes got up to leave. I immediately stood up to thank him and shook his hand.

"Thank you for contacting me and sharing your experience," I said as I reached my hand out to shake.

"That's fine; I just felt like talking about it. I haven't said anything to anyone about this; my sister is the only other person who knows and that is because she was there with me when it happened."

"Take care of yourself; if you need anything please don't hesitate to contact me," I said as he made his way to the exit. I turned back to my coffee and to the notes that I had taken. I knew that what he and his wife had gone through was something that I too was familiar with, having experienced things like that myself. I haven't heard anything more from him and I don't anticipate it even after the release of this book.

Afterwards

This experience may seem like something out of a horror movie, but unfortunately, these kinds of things happen all too frequently. It is a part of paranormal research that often goes unspoken about. When we read about these kinds of cases, it is hard to imagine how it must have felt or what it was truly like—especially if we have never experienced anything like it before in our own lives. These kinds of cases have started to come out into the public more and more over the last five to ten years, and I am not sure if it is because they are becoming more and more frequent, or if the general attitudes towards them have changed.

The talking board was the catalyst for everything that happened; coupled with the emotional troubles and stress that the married couple was going through. Unfortunately, when the door is opened and something is invited to come through it; it can have devastating effects on all of those involved.

Fortunately, there are a number of these kinds of incidents where, as a result of the experience, the family or individual who experiences them comes out of it more spiritually connected and is stronger in their resolve. It is very sad to see someone be so deeply affected in a way that prevents them from ever truly recovering from it. In the case of this man's wife, the experience has left her traumatized and emotionally unstable. I wish her well and hope that they both someday will find peace.

Portal Experiments—Part II

The summer was in full swing. It was entering August of 2006 and the portal experiments had been going on since December of 2005. The weekend that my brother and I conducted those beginning experiments had been on the Fourth of July weekend. That was the last real time that I or anyone from the group carried out any experiments of that type in the house, and it wasn't too long after that, that we had stopped any formal investigations from going on in the house. The activity in the West Chester home had escalated to the point where things were starting to happen at the homes of some of the members of the group.

CCPRS was about to enter an extremely busy time; starting with the Phoenixville Public Library investigation that took place on August 12th, 2006. (Read about the Library investigation in *Ghosts of Valley Forge and Phoenixville*). We would stay busy with investigations, lectures, classes, fundraisers, documentaries, and all kinds of things that would go well into mid November and end our 2006 season with our investigation at Eastern State Penitentiary. (Read about the ESP investigation in *Philadelphia Haunts*.) During and all through this time, the activity at the house had turned from benign to somewhat menacing. It was during this time that something very strong began to make its presence known to me, my wife, and other members of the group.

My wife and I began to wake up nightly at about 3:30 in the morning. It was always something that would wake us up—a noise, a dream, or the presence of something else in the room. We began to realize that something was starting to test us to see what we could take. I hated to admit it, but the thought that something inhuman, or possibly demonic, was starting to make itself known was a bit overwhelming. I had had experiences with things of this nature before and I knew that it would take a tremendous amount of strength, willpower, and faith to get through it.

The animals in the house seemed to be tormented by something unseen. The dog would constantly run and hide under the end table or stay nearby at our feet. She would be laying on the floor and suddenly jump up and yelp as though something had just touched her or stepped on her. This unfortunately happened many times and made her very nervous.

There was one particular experience that I had in late October of that year that made me realize that whatever it was in the house was not friendly—and was very deceiving. Late one morning, I was still in bed sleeping. My wife had already gotten up and left the house for work. I didn't have to work until the evening, so I'd decided to let myself sleep in.

I had woken up several times throughout the morning to the feeling that something was in the room with me. I was lying on my side, with my back to the door, and I had just started to fall back asleep when the door opened. I was half in a dream and half awake when it happened, but I know that through previous experiences and other cases of this type, that what I was experiencing was real, and potentially very dangerous.

I then had something climb into the bed and get up against me at my back. I could feel it pressing against me and I heard a female voice calling to me, beckoning me to roll over to see her. At first, I thought it was my wife trying to get me up, but instantly I remembered that she wasn't in the house and that this wasn't my wife who was having some form of contact with me.

I awoke more and more, but still the presence was there, calling out to me. I immediately began to pray and to tell myself that this wasn't my wife and that, whatever it was, I was not going to look at it.

The room got very cold and the presence was no longer beckoning me, but had changed. I prayed harder and tried not to listen to it or acknowledge it in anyway. It then, without notice, vanished and was gone from the room.

I sat up and looked around the room, shuddering at the idea of what it might have been that was just there with me.

Other incidents would occur as well. The shadows in the house became more prevalent and we would start to hear knocking at the front door or front window. When we would go to answer the door, no one was actually there—or at least no one we could see.

I had talked to Kyle on our CCPRS team about the situation. He had been an investigator for quite some time and had been a member of another group that had investigated several cases with activity like we were having in our house. He could tell right away upon entering our home that something was going on that was very different than the usual kinds of activity that had been displayed in the past.

My wife and I realized very quickly that we needed to be stronger in our faith and resolve. Unfortunately, we had both been through something very similar to this several years before while living in Philadelphia. I knew that I had to be more careful and to take a stand against whatever it was that was making its presence known now.

Over the next few weeks, things calmed down a bit. Our usual "house guests" were still present, but the feeling of something darker and potentially menacing let up. Christine and Jack from ECHO (East Coast Hauntings Organization) were the last formal investigators to come through the house and do a walk-through or investigation. We'd stopped investigating at the house with our group and no longer trained new members there in an attempt to let things quiet down a bit. It had become a bit overwhelming for my wife and I to deal with on a daily basis.

Over the course of the next year to the present, November 7, 2007 (at the time I am writing this), the house would remain very active. During the last few months, there has been a dramatic increase in the presence of shadows and other visual-based phenomena. The first floor of the house was generally much quieter than the second floor, but there has been an increase in activity there as well. Fortunately, the darker presence has not been active and has been fairly quiet in recent months. We have stayed vigilant and taken greater care to try to keep it from coming back.

Afterwards

It has been a year and a half since I set out to write this book. I've encountered many haunting challenges along the way, but I was able to get through them to bring together the stories and experiences for this book. It seems that there are more and more people everyday coming out with occurrences that they have had at one time or another in their lives relating to the world of the paranormal. Is the attitude towards this area of understanding changing? Is it becoming more acceptable and more believable?

I find that those who have experienced even the smallest of paranormal activities are believers, yet the skeptics remain strong no matter what is presented before them. I have accepted that fact and have given up long ago trying to prove that the skeptics are wrong. It doesn't mean that I won't continue to try and collect evidence and conduct myself in a way that will hopefully contribute positively to this work as a whole. I sincerely hope that this area of research continues to grow and flourish, and that, someday, some major breakthroughs are brought forth in technology, methodology, and theory used in conducting paranormal research. I ultimately know that it is a matter of time before something like this might occur. I encourage those who have had experiences to be willing to share them, because you will find out very quickly that you are not alone.

We have explored various kinds of paranormal activity and have seen how, sometimes, in rare cases, it can be dangerous to those directly involved—but again, those are the more rare and extreme of cases. The excitement and thrill of a paranormal experience can lead us to wanting more, but we must take care. To quote the famous saying: "Be careful for what you wish for; you just might get it."

The following section, I've prepared for the Chester County Paranormal Research Society in Pennsylvania and have offered if to other paranormal groups for the development of their groups and the education of their contacts. It also appears in training materials for new investigators for our group members.

Please visit
www.ChesterCountyprs.com
for more information.

Glossary

Air Probe Thermometer

A thermometer with an external probe that is capable of taking instant measurements of the air temperature.

Anomalous field

A field that can not be explained or ruled out by various possibilities, that can be a representation of spirit or paranormal energy present.

Apparition

A transparent form of a human or animal, a spirit.

Artificial field

A field that is caused by electrical outlets, appliances, etc.

Aural Enhancer

A listening device that enhances or amplifies audio signals. i.e., Orbitor Bionic Ear.

Automatic writing

The act of a spirit guiding a human agent in writing a message that is brought through by the spirit.

Base readings

The readings taken at the start of an investigation and are used as a means of comparing other readings taken later during the course of the investigation.

Demonic Haunting

A haunting that is caused by an inhuman or subhuman energy or spirit.

Dowsing Rods

A pair of L-shaped rods or a single Y-shaped rod, used to detect the presence of what the person using them is trying to find.

Electro-static generator

A device that electrically charges the air often used in paranormal investigations/research as a means to contribute to the materialization of paranormal or spiritual energy.

ELF

Extremely Low Frequency.

ELF Meter/EMF Meter

A device that measures electric and magnetic fields.

EMF

Electro Magnetic Field.

EVP

Electronic Voice Phenomena. The act of catching disembodied voices or imprints of paranormal events onto audio recording devices.

False positive

Something that is being interpreted as paranormal within a picture or video and is, in fact, a natural occurrence or defect of the equipment used.

Gamera

A 35mm film camera connected with a motion detector that is housed in a weather proof container and takes a picture when movement is detected. Made by Silver Creek Industries.

Geiger Counter

A device that measures gamma and x-ray radiation.

Infra Red

An invisible band of radiation at the lower end of the visible light spectrum. With wavelengths from 750 nm to 1 mm, infrared starts at the end of the microwave spectrum and ends at the beginning of visible light. Infrared transmission typically requires an unobstructed line of sight between transmitter and receiver. Widely used in most audio and video remote controls, infrared transmission is also used for wireless connections between computer devices and a variety of detectors.

Intelligent haunting

A haunting of a spirit or other entity that has the ability to interact with the living and do things that can make its presence known.

Matrixing

This is a phenomenon where the brain attempts to make order out of chaos in a pattern or design, photograph or other image where something is seen that in fact might not be there. For example: seeing a face in a picture when in fact one is not there.

Milli-gauss

Unit of measurement, measures in 1000th of a gauss and is named for the famous German mathematician, Karl Gauss.

Orbs

Anomalous spherical shapes that appear on video and still photography.

Pendulum

A pointed item that is hung on the end of a string or chain and is used as a means of contacting spirits. An individual will hold the item and let it hang from the finger tips. The individual will ask questions aloud and the pendulum answers by moving.

Poltergeist haunting

A haunting that has two sides, but same kinds of activity in common. Violent outbursts of activity with doors and windows slamming shut, items being thrown across a room and things being knocked off of surfaces. Poltergeist hauntings are usually focused around a specific individual who resides or works at the location of the activity reported, and, in some cases, when the person is not present at the location, activity does not occur. A poltergeist haunting may be the cause of a human agent or spirit/energy that may be present at the location.

Portal

An opening in the realm of the paranormal that is a gateway between one dimension and the next. A passageway for spirits to come and go through. See also Vortex.

Residual haunting

A haunting that is an imprint of an event or person that plays itself out like a loop until the energy that causes it has burned itself out.

Scrying

The act of eliciting information with the use of a pendulum from spirits.

Sleep Seizures

Also known as a Focal Seizure, this is in between sleep and consciousness when the mind is awake and conscious but the body is still asleep. The sensation of a buzzing or electric sound felt or heard, the body is paralyzed, auditory hallucinations and sometimes visual hallucinations can occur.

Strobe Light

This is a light that is set on a variable timer that flashes in quick successions and is controlled by a dial that can speed up or slow down the rate at which the light flashes.

Table Tipping

A form of spirit communication, the act of a table being used as a form of contact. Individuals will sit around a table and lightly place there fingertips on the edge of the table and elicit contact with a spirit. The Spirit will respond by "tipping" or moving the table.

Talking Boards

A board used as a means of communicating with a spirit. Also known as a Quija Board.

Tone Generator

A device used to produce specific audio frequencies. This kind of device is often used as a test gauge for calibrating and troubleshooting certain types of audio equipment.

Video Feedback Loop

This is type of visual distortion that is produced when a video camera is connected directly into a television and pointed back directly into the television, thus causing a loop that feedbacks into itself.

Vortex

A place or situation regarded as drawing into its center all that surrounds it.

White Noise

A random noise signal that has the same sound energy level at all frequencies.

Equipment Explanations

In this section, the Chester County Paranormal Research Society looks at the application and benefits of equipment used on investigations with greater detail. The equipment used for an investigation plays a vital role in the ability to collect objective evidence and helps to determine what *is* and *is not* paranormal activity. But a key point to be made here is: the investigator is the most important tool on any investigation. With that said, let us now take a look at the main pieces of equipment used during an investigation...

The Geiger Counter

The Geiger counter is device that measures radiation. A "Geiger counter" usually contains a metal tube with a thin metal wire along its middle. The space in between them is sealed off and filled with a suitable gas and with the wire at about +1000 volts relative to the tube.

An ion or electron penetrating the tube (or an electron knocked out of the wall by X-rays or gamma rays) tears electrons off atoms in the gas. Because of the high positive voltage of the central wire, those electrons are then attracted to it. They gain energy that collide with atoms and release more electrons, until the process snowballs into an "avalanche", producing an easily detectable pulse of current. With a suitable filling gas, the flow of electricity stops by itself, or else the electrical circuitry can help stop it.

The instrument was called a "counter" because every particle passing it produced an identical pulse, allowing particles to be counted, usually electronically. But it did not tell anything about their identity or energy, except that they must have sufficient energy to penetrate the walls of the counter.

The Geiger counter is used in paranormal research to measure the background radiation at a location. The working theory in this field is that paranormal activity can effect the background radiation. In some cases, it will increase the radiation levels and in other cases it will decrease the levels.

Digital and 35mm Film Cameras

The camera is an imperative piece of equipment that enabled us to gather objective evidence during a case. Some of the best evidence presented from cases of paranormal activity over the years has been because of photographs taken. If you own your own digital camera or 35mm film camera, you need to be fully aware of what the cameras abilities and limitations are. Digital cameras have been at the center of great debate in the field of paranormal research over the years.

The earlier incarnations of digital cameras were full of inherent problems and notorious for creating "false positive" pictures. A "false positive" picture is a picture that has anomalous elements within the picture that are the result of a camera defect or other natural occurrence. There are many pictures scattered about the internet that claim to be of true paranormal activity, but in fact they are "false positives." Orbs, defined as anomalous paranormal energy that can show up as balls of light or streaks in still photography or video, are the most controversial pictures of paranormal energy in the field. There are so many theories (good and bad) about the origin of orbs and what they are. Every picture in the CCPRS collection that has an orb—or orbs—are not presented in a way that state that they are absolutely paranormal of nature. I have yet to capture an orb photo that made me feel certain that in fact it is of a paranormal nature.

If you use your own camera, understand that your camera is vital. I encourage all members who own their own cameras to do research on the make and model of the camera and see what other consumers are saying about them. Does the manufacturer give any info regarding possible defects or design flaws with that particular model? Understanding your camera will help to rule out the possibility of interpreting a "false positive" for an authentic picture of paranormal activity.

Video Cameras

The video camera is also a fundamental tool in the investigation as another way for collecting objective evidence that can support the proof of paranormal activity. The video camera can be used in various ways during the investigation. It can be set on a tripod and left in a location where paranormal activity has been reported. It can also be used as a hand-held camera and the investigator will take it with them during their walk through investigation as a means of documenting to hopefully capture anomalous activity on tape. Infra-Red technology has become a feature on most consumer level video cameras and depending on the manufacturer can be called "night shot" or "night alive." What this technology does is allow us to use the camera in zero light. Most cameras with this feature will add a green tint or haze to the camera when it is being used in this mode. A video camera with this ability holds great appeal to the paranormal investigator.

EMF/ELF Meters
EMF=Electro Magnetic Frequency
ELF=Extremely Low Frequency

What is an EMF/ELF meter? Good question. The EMF/ELF meter is a meter that measures Electric and Magnetic fields in an AC or DC current field. It measures in a unit of measurement called "milli-gauss," named for the famous German mathematician, Karl Gauss. Most meters will measure in a range of 1-5 or 1-10 milli-gauss. The reason that EMF meters are used in paranormal research is because of the theory that a spirit or paranormal energy can add to the energy field when it is materializing or is present in a location. The theory says that, typically, an energy that measures between 3-7 milli-gauss may be of a paranormal origin. This doesn't mean that an artificial field can't also measure within this range. That is why we take base readings and make maps noting where artificial fields occur. The artificial fields are a direct result of electricity, i.e. wiring, appliances, light switches, electrical outlets, circuit breakers, high voltage power lines, sub-stations, etc.

The Earth emits a naturally occurring magnetic field all around us and has an effect on paranormal activity. Geomagnetic storm activity can also have a great influence on paranormal activity. For more information on this kind of phenomena visit: www.noaa.sec.com.

There are many different types of EMF meters; and each one, although it measures with the same unit of measurement, may react differently. An EMF meter can range from anywhere to $12.00 to $1,000.00 or more depending on the quality and features that it has. Most meters are measuring the AC (alternating current, the type of fields created by man-made electricity) fields and some can measure DC (direct current-naturally occurring fields, batteries also fall into the category of DC) fields. The benefit of having a meter that can measure DC fields is that they will automatically filter out the artificial fields created by AC fields and can pick up more naturally occurring electro magnetic fields. Some of the higher-tech EMF meters are so sensitive that they can pick up the fields generated by living beings. The EMF meter was originally designed to measure the earth's magnetic fields and also to measure the fields created by electrical an artificial means.

There have been various studies over the years about the long term effects of individuals living in or near high fields. There has been much controversy as to whether or not long term exposure to high fields can lead to cancer. It has been proven though that no matter what, long term exposure to high fields can be harmful to your health. The ability to locate these high fields within a private residence or business is vital to the investigation. We may offer suggestions to the client as to possible solutions for dealing with high fields. The wiring in a home or business can greatly affect the possibility of high fields. If the wiring is old and/or not shielded correctly, it can emit high fields that may affect the ability to correctly notate any anomalous fields that may be present.

Audio Recording Equipment

Audio recording equipment is used for conducting EVP (Electronic Voice Phenomena) research and experiments. What is an EVP? An EVP is a phenomenon where paranormal voices or sounds can be captured with audio recording devices. The theory is that the activity will imprint directly onto the device or tape, but has not been proven to be an absolute fact. The use of an external microphone is essential when conducting EVP experiments with analog recording equipment. The internal microphone on an analog tape recorder can pick up the background noise of the working parts within the tape recorder and can taint the evidence as a whole. Most digital recorders are quiet enough to use the internal microphone, but as a general rule of thumb, we do not use them. An external microphone will be used always. Another theory about EVP research is that an authentic EVP will happen within the range 250-400hz. This is a lower frequency range and isn't easily heard by the human ear, and the human voice does not emit in this range. EVP is rarely heard at the moment it happens—it is usually revealed during the playback and analysis portion of the investigation.

Thermometers

The use of a thermometer in an investigation goes without saying. This is how we monitor the temperature changes during the course of an investigation. CCPRS is currently using Digital thermometers with remote sensors as a way to set up a perimeter and to notate any changes in a stationary location of an investigation. The Air-probe thermometer can take "real time" readings that are instantly accurate. This is the more appropriate thermometer for measuring air temperature and "cold spots" that may be caused by the presence of paranormal phenomena. The IR Non-contact thermometer is the most misused thermometer in the field of paranormal research. CCPRS does not own or use IR Non-contact thermometers for this reason. The IR (infra-red) Non-contact thermometer is meant for measuring surface temperatures from a remote location. It shoots an infrared beam out to an object and bounces to the unit and gives the temperature reading. I have seen, first hand, investigators using this thermometer as a way to measure air temperature. NO, this is not correct! Enough said. In an email conversation that I have had with Grant Wilson from TAPS, he has said that, "Any change in temperature that can't be measured with your hand is not worth notating…"

Haunted and Interesting Places
In and Around West Chester

West Chester

Chester County Historical Society
The Ground Round—Route 3, West Chester Pike
Everhart Grove—100 South Brandywine Street
Marshall Square Park—200 East Marshall Street
Hemlock Alley
Ramsey Hall, West Chester University
Neilds Street Railroad Crossing
Intersection of High and Market Streets
Chestnut Grove Cemetery (off Gay Street)
The site of the old gallows (Paoli Pike and Gay Street)
Nields Street Railroad Crossing
Route 52 and Rosedale Avenue
Hollinger Field House, West Chester University

Spring City

Pennhurst State Hospital and School

Parkesburg

The Stotsville Inn

Downingtown

Twin Tunnels of Downingtown
Route 322 West towards Downingtown from West Chester
Sawmill Road (The Gates of Hell)
Downingtown Library

Phoenixville

Phoenixville Public Library
Reeves Park (The park across from the Phoenixville Library)
The Mansion House
Wolfgang Books

Philadelphia

Fort Mifflin
Eastern State Penitentiary
Philadelphia Water Works Museum/Art Museum area

Brandywine/Chadds Ford

Brandywine Battlefield—Ticking Tombstone

Valley Forge

General Wayne Statue
George Washington Headquarters
George Washington Memorial Chapel
The General Wayne Inn—625 Montgomery Avenue, Merion, PA 19066

West Chester History Outline
The First 200 years

Pre-West Chester History

Mid 1700's
Three tracts of land came together on the border between Goshen Township and Bradford Township.

1753

By 1753, the road from Wilmington to the Valley (known as Wilmington Road or Valley Road) had been laid down (modern-day High Street).

Turk's Head didn't spring to life until the Philadelphia Road (modern-day West Chester Pike, Route 3) and Wilmington Road were laid out.

The first public building to be laid out was at the intersection of these two roads and was built by John Eachus. John gave 150 of the 250-acre tract to his son, Phineas.

1761

Turk's Head Tavern—In 1761, Phineas petitioned the courts for a tavern license and was granted the license in 1762.

1768

The 150-acre tract was sold in a sheriff's sale to Isaiah Matlack.

1769

John Hooper acquired the land and the Tavern.

(Before) 1770

A schoolhouse was built on the west side of Wilmington Road. The schoolyard was located behind the building.

1774

Jacob James became the Tavern keeper.

September 15, 1777

Wounded American troops arrived in Turk's Head, escorted by their British captors after the battle of the Brandywine. The Tavern was converted into a makeshift hospital.

1793

The first Roman Catholic congregation was established in West Chester.

1799
The town of West Chester was elevated to a borough and the West Chester Fire Company was founded.

1804
The West Chester Post Office was established.

1805
Hannah Miller became the first criminal execution to take place in West Chester.

1814
The Bank of West Chester was founded on High Street.

1823
The first sidewalks of West Chester were laid in brick.

1829-1830
Gay and Church Streets became paved for the first time.

1830
Edward Williams was executed at the gallows.

1831
West Chester built a new market on Market Street.

1832
Railway lines were constructed from West Chester to Malvern.

1833
The Good Will Fire Company was founded.

1834
Charles Bowman was executed at the gallows.

1838

The Fame Fire Company was founded.

1841

West Chester received its first waterworks system on land purchased from Anthony Bolmar and Joshua Hoopes. The reservoir and pumping station were located at Marshall Square.

1845

Jabez Boyd was executed at the gallows.

1846

The present day court house was built.

1850s

During the 1850s several "underground railroad" routes passed from Kennett, East Bradford, West Chester, and Willistown, on to Philadelphia.

1851

West Chester received its first telegraph connection.

1851

George Pharoah was executed at the gallows.

1852

West Chester received its first gas light company.

1857

The sidewalks of West Chester were nearly complete and laid in brick.

1858

The Pennsylvania Railroad took over the railway line between West Chester and Malvern, and the first train reached West Chester from Philadelphia via Media.

1862

Chester County's population reached 77,000, and the state of Pennsylvania had hit 2,900,000.

1871

The Villa Maria Academy was founded by the Sisters of the Immaculate Heart of Mary. The State Normal School also opened in the same year.

1872

The newspaper *The Daily Local News* was founded.

1883

The first telephones in West Chester were installed. Among the first customers were the *Morning Republican*, Hoopes Brothers & Thomas, Dr. John R. McClurg, S. A. Kirk, Jerome Gray, *The Daily Local*, and *The Village Recorder*.

1884

There were only fifty telephones in West Chester. Also in 1884, the West Chester Women's Christian Temperance Union was founded.

1885

The Edison Electric Illuminating Company of West Chester was established.

1887

The West Chester Board of Trade was established.

1889

Typhoid fever strikes on the east side of West Chester.

1892

Scarlet fever strikes two families on East Nields Street.

1893

The Chester County Hospital becomes established in a pair of buildings on the north side of Marshall Square.

1894

Water pipes were laid from East Nields Street north along South Adams Street for a single square.

1899

West Chester had almost 140 long-distance telephones with lines that reached Chicago and Boston.

1901

There were 175 telephones in West Chester.

1905

The first automobile owner in West Chester was Joseph H. Sager, who bought a *Locomobile* in New York City for $850.

1912

The Baldwin Electric Shop was founded by Walter C. Baldwin at 20 S. Church Street.

1914

The Villa Maria Academy moved from West Chester to its present location at Immaculata and was chartered by the state of Pennsylvania in 1921.

1918

The Boy Scouts were chartered in Chester County. Their headquarters was located in the Farmers and Mechanics Building in West Chester.

1927

The Girl Scouts were chartered in Chester County at the suggestion of Mrs. Herbert Hoover, following a "tea" held at the home (named "Greystone") of Mrs. P. M. Sharples.

1931

The Goose Creek Fire took place when a train derailed, spilling flammable contents into the creek and was struck ablaze by an unknowing citizen who flung a match into the creek.

1944

Greenfield Park was built in Riggtown on land donated to the borough by realtor Harry F. Taylor.

1952

The first diesel locomotive reached West Chester.

1953

The Nields Street Railroad crossing accident happens, killing everyone in the car. It was considered one of the worst railroad accidents in West Chester history.

Bibliography & Web Site Resources

Print

Daily Local News. "West Chester Transportation; PA. RR 1940-1954." Chester County Historical Society clippings file, June 6, 1953.

Guiley, Rosemary Ellen. *Encyclopedia of Ghosts and Spirits*. Checkmark Books; 2 edition (October 2000)

Harper, Douglas R. *West Chester to 1865: that elegant & notorious place* (Unknown Binding). Published: 1999 Chester County Historical Society, West Chester, PA.

Kaku, Michio. *Hyperspace: A Scientific Odyssey Through Parallel Universes, Time Warps, and the 10th Dimension.* Anchor (February 1, 1995).

Roseberry, D. P. *Ghosts of Valley Forge and Phoenixville*. Atglen, Pennsylvania: Schiffer Publishing, 2006

Rupert Sargent Holland. *Mad Anthony, The Story of Anthony Wayne,* New York & London: The Century Company, 1931.

Sarro, Katharine. *Philadelphia Haunts*. Atglen, Pennsylvania: Schiffer Publishing, 2008

Sarro, Mark & Michele Rainey. *Chester County Paranormal Research Society Hand Book*. West Chester, Pennsylvania, 2005, 2006.

Walton and Brumbaugh. *Stories of Pennsylvania*. Martin Grove Brumbaugh, American book Co., Pennsylvania, 1897.

Rodebaugh, Paul A. West Chester, The First 200 Years: 1799-1999. West Chester Bicentennial History Committee, 1999.

Web Site Resources

Chester County Historical Society. http://www.cchs-pa.org/index.php

Chester County Links. www.chestercountylinks.com

Chester County Night School (Deb Estep's paranormal classes). http://www.chestercountynightschool.org/courses/personal.htm

Chester County Paranormal Research Society (CCPRS). www.chestercountyprs.com

East Coast Hauntings Organization (ECHO). www.ghostecho.com

Ghost Seekers.Former members of CCPRS; Cindy and Ruth's group: www.theghostseekers.com

NOAA (Space Weather). www.spaceweather.com

Paranormal Research equipment and supplies. www.ghosthunterstore.com

Prairie Ghosts. www.prairieghosts.com

Riggtown History home page. http://courses.wcupa.edu/jones/his480/riggtown.htm

Schiffer Books. www.schifferbooks.com

West Chester Events. www.westchesterevents.com

West Chester Fire Department. www.famefireco.org

Index of Places and Stories

Everhart Grove, 100 South Brandywine Street, West Chester, Pennsylvania, Page 69

"Amongst the Trees"- A woman retells the account of an encounter with a shadow person while walking her dog in the park.

Hemlock Alley, (Between Barnard and Miner Streets) from Everhart Grove to Church Street, West Chester, Pennsylvania, Page 76

"The Alley"– The shadow person sighted by man on his way home from work.

Undisclosed West Chester Home, West Chester, Pennsylvania, Page 77

"Shadow in the Doorway"– The anonymous tale of a man's encounter with a shadow person in his home.

Marshall Square Park, 200 East Marshall Street, West Chester, Pennsylvania, Page 78

"The Pentagram Trees" – A couple walking home from dinner meets with a shadow person lurking in the park. The location of the grouping of trees that resemble a Pentagram.